# Life Passages

*When Age Point Aspects and Dreams Coincide*

John D. Grove

Knutsford, England

First published in the U.K. in 2017 by HopeWell

HopeWell
130 Grove Park, Knutsford
Cheshire WA16 8QD, U.K.



Edited by Barry Hopewell & Sue Lewis.

Cover art: Dream-inspired works by John Grove.

Astrological charts produced using Cathar software, www.catharsoftware.com.

ISBN 978-0-9956736-1-8

## Dedicated to

This book is dedicated to my adult children, Thomas Galen Grove and Miranda Lynn Nelli who have always been subjected to my obsession with their dreams and have provided valuable insight to the creation of this work.

## Acknowledgements

Thank you to Barry Hopewell for publishing this book, and to Sue Lewis for giving editorial assistance and encouraging its creation. Thanks to my wife Judy for her steadfast positive thoughts. To the volunteers who contributed their dreams for use in my research and to those who provided their astrological data for inclusion into initiation rituals described in Chapter 2.

# Contents

# Preface

I was very pleased to be asked to write the preface to *Life Passages*, in which John Grove synthesizes age progression through the twelve houses of the horoscope—the method devised by Bruno and Louise Huber—with the eight stages of psycho-social development identified by Erik Erikson—the German-born, American psychotherapist who coined the phrase, 'identity crisis'. John applies these methods to the processing of personal material that arises from within at strategic times of change accompanied by vivid dreams.

John is a psychotherapist with extensive experience of working with veterans and interpreting dreams, who has a *Diploma in Astrological Psychology* of the Astrological Psychology Association and is ideally qualified to write this sequel to his earlier work, *Dreams and Astrological Psychology: The Way through the Maze of the Unconscious. Life Passages* is a more tightly constructed volume that concentrates on establishing connections between the Life Clock of astrological psychology, developmental psychological profiles, and dreams that represent a turning point in the lives of individuals. A selection of revealing case studies illustrates John's findings.

The quest to identify correspondences between astrological significators and dreams has a long history, dating back to classical and biblical eras. Notably, the Renaissance astrologer Girolamo Cardano kept a dream diary on which the psychotherapist C G Jung gave a series of lectures in the 1930s. Cardano's dreams stimulated him intellectually, and he looked for clues to understanding the immediate future, so he took a different perspective from Jung, Huber, and Grove, who use astrological and dream interpretation to guide the individual towards wholeness and strength.

The Huber Life Clock adds all-important timing to events in the outer and inner lives of individuals. Its location in house and sign, and its relationship to specific planets can help client and counsellor to make sense of images that emerge in dreams at pivotal moments, and connect them with the motivational patterns shown on an accurately drawn astrological chart. As well as being rooted in esoteric wisdom and attuned to the hermetic maxim 'as above, so below', astrological psychology's birth chart is a precise psychological map, and its method is assimilated with the psychosynthesis of Roberto Assagioli, as reiterated by Louise Huber in her interview with Verena Bachmann

(2003). This volume emphasizes the importance of using visual and symbolic language to develop a healthy ego in preparation for the spiritual path, and images that arise from the unconscious in dreams can be assimilated into consciousness with the help of astrological interpretation.

Following the Introduction, Chapter 1 presents the seventy-two-year cycle of the Life Clock with its loud and soft phases and rhythms, together with psycho-social tasks from infancy to late adulthood. Notwithstanding the acknowledged need to revise Erikson's dated definitions of sexual identity in a contemporary context, overall the combined framework of reference stands up well. This first chapter culminates with an analysis of an important dream the author had at the age of 24, just after his age point entered the fifth house. At this time, he finally left behind the security of the family home and took a challenging job overseas. John is at his very best when illustrating his points with case histories, and giving honest portrayals of himself and those who are willing to share their experience with a wider public.

Chapter 2 takes a closer look at life tasks, and emphasizes how necessary it is to differentiate between wants, desires, and self-gratification on the one hand, and what one actually needs to do to develop a healthy ego on the other. The threefold personality of Huber astrology and Abraham Maslow's hierarchy of needs provide helpful tools for working in a supportive therapeutic environment. Tensions between inherited behaviour traits and environmental pressure are explored in some depth, with a couple of illustrative case histories, testing the ego as it strengthens and prepares for initiation.

In Chapter 3, the focus is on dream patterns, how to create the right environment for capturing dreams, and how to assimilate such ephemeral material from unknown worlds into waking consciousness. This sets the scene for the six case histories of dreams at critical moments in life, featured in Chapter 4.

The final chapter sums up the advantages of using the Huber method of astrological consultation with dream interpretation to achieve personal integrity and psychosynthesis, preparing the way for a spiritual path, a perspective on life supported by astrological interpretation that I fully endorse.

Sue Lewis, MA (Western Esotericism), DipAPI, DFAstrolS
7 April 2017

# Introduction

*When the moon is in the seventh House*
*And Jupiter aligned with Mars*
*Then peace will guide the planets*
*And love will steer the stars.*
*This is the dawning of the Age of Aquarius.*
*Age of Aquarius!*

*5th Dimension, Robert Westerfield,*
*Sharon De Adel, Daniel Gibson*

Astrology covers much more than the daily descriptions of the Sun signs that one reads in the newspaper. It actually has nothing to do with fortune telling, although that is the popular conception. In fact, *"Astrology has always been concerned with something much more for it really deals with the human psyche and the paths to self-awareness".*[i] As a practicing psychotherapist, I have been studying the psycho-social issues facing my clients, and I have used astrology as a frame of reference for the developmental model of psycho-social opportunities and crises confronting the individual as he/she ages throughout life.

Developmental psychology is the scientific study of how and why human beings change over the course of their lives, starting with childhood and going through youth, adolescence, young adulthood, mature adulthood and elderly adulthood.[ii] The study of human behavior starts from birth and defines the psycho-social tasks of development from the cradle to the grave.[iii]

Astrological Psychology's Age Point progression deals with the psychological development of the human being throughout the life cycle, starting with birth (using an accurate time and place of birth as essential data), by studying the traversing of what is called an Age Point (AP) through the houses of the horoscope. AP progression is a method of highlighting problems and opportunities as the individual confronts the phases of growth that he/she experiences, based on the environmental issues that are manifested through the twelve houses of the horoscope.

As Joyce Hopewell, Principal Emeritus of the Astrological Psychology Association, enthusiastically points out: *"If you had a tool which identified precisely where you are now on your life journey, and which took into account the psychological and developmental phase you're currently moving through, together with what this means for you as a unique individual, wouldn't you want to use it?"* [iv]

Erik Erikson defined the ego as the *"'inner institution' evolved to safeguard that order within individuals on which all outer order depends".* [v] Jung came up with the idea of ego as *"a complex of representations which constitutes the centre of my field of consciousness and appears to possess a very high degree of continuity and identity."* [vi] Huber defined the ego or personality planets of the Sun, Moon, and Saturn as the structure of our personal power on three levels: mental, emotional and physical, respectively. Huber would agree with Jung and Erikson that the ego is the conscious element in the psyche.

Astrological Psychology theory encompasses the complete individual because it proposes a three-fold personality development as one individualizes. Huber's conceptualization of the integration of the three-fold personality with the preferred ego planet (Sun, Moon or Saturn) mediating between two levels: the tool planets or instinct (Venus, Mars, Mercury and Jupiter); and the spiritual planets, conscience or ideal ego (Uranus, Neptune and Pluto). The three tiers have a parallel psychic structure with psychoanalytic theory's ego, id and superego.

Jung describes four psychic functions of consciousness—thinking, feeling, sensation and intuition—which he believed are constitutionally present in every individual: *"all men constitutionally possess all four functions and [their development] determines which one would undergo the most profound development and differentiation to become the dominant function."* [vii] The process of differentiation for Jung is called individualism, which is development in line with ego attachments and social norms, including occupational identity. For Bruno Huber, the integration of the strongest of the ego planets—the mental (Sun), emotional (Moon) or physical (Saturn)—determines which will lead the way for integration of the personality by becoming the strongest force in the personality for differentiation. For Roberto Assagioli, the founder of Psychosynthesis, the process of integrating this personality, called psychosynthesis, *"leads us toward a new and creative rebirth of the real inner human being."* [viii] Assagioli's concept of integration is based on meeting the real needs of the individual, which I assume are those needs for physiological stasis, safety, belonging/love, self-esteem, and self-actualization, paralleled by Abraham Maslow's basic needs.

But that is not the end of psychological growth. Individuation is the process of becoming whole by integration of opposite functions of the psyche as one matures. *"By activating the contents of the unconscious, such an effort eases the tension between pairs of opposites (i.e. thinking vs. feeling, for example) and makes possible a living knowledge of their structure... Thus self-realization, both in the individual and in the extrapersonal, collective sense, becomes a moral decision, and it is this moral decision which lends force to the process of self-fulfillment that Jung calls individuation... Jung believed that the spiritual appears in the psyche also as an instinct; indeed as a real passion, and that the spiritual and religious need that is innate in the psyche unique to man is the essential part of Jung's theory which distinguishes it from all others and determines the prospective-synthetic direction".*[ix] Roberto Assagioli has also included the spiritual or transpersonal development as an important and necessary phase of growth of the human being. I believe that by using dreams from the unconscious to correlate with AP progression we are led on the path to individuation as we understand how to resolve the psychological opposites as tensions in our psyches.

Age Point progression in Astrological Psychology is a time-based method in which the passage of a point called the Age Point traverses all twelve houses of the zodiac. It starts with House 1 when the child is born, takes six years to travel through the first house and each subsequent house. One full revolution around the whole chart takes seventy-two years. Below is a chart with the twelve houses; 0 is where the child starts her AP progression in the first house of the Life Clock (Figure 1). At age 6, she is moving into the second house, and

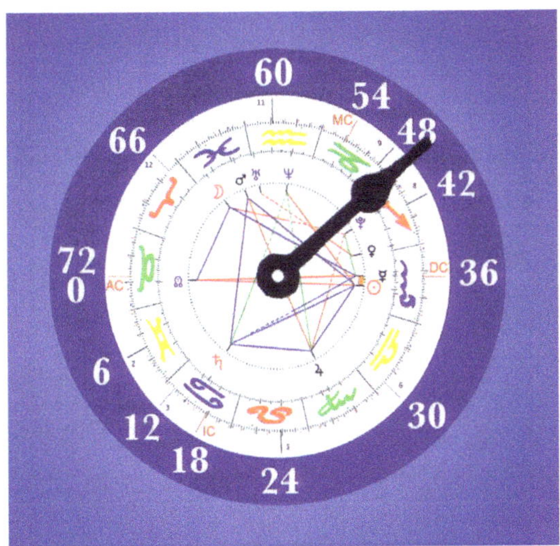


**Figure 1. The Life Clock**

into successive houses, each one traversing six years until the whole life cycle is completed at age 72. Then it starts over again in the first house, moving through each house every six years—2nd house at 78, third house at 84 etc…[x]

As the AP highlights sensitive points in the horoscope, certain challenges, issues and opportunities confront the growing human being. This process continues throughout life and determines behavioral outcomes and consequences, as one experiences the world through the lens of the twelve astrological houses representing a systematic involvement with the environment: *"The twelve houses or life arenas, in the life experience of man/woman are the most important developmental element of astrological psychology. They are the reference system to the real world and they show the psychological processes which occur constantly between the individual and his environment".*[xi] Below is a depiction of the psychological experience of the AP traversing through the twelve houses, the ages involved, and the psychological interpretation for the individual involved (Figure 2).[xii]

| House | Age | Phase |
|---|---|---|
| 1st | 0 - 6 | Formation of the "I" |
| 2nd | 6 - 12 | Creation of life and awareness of possessions |
| 3rd | 12 – 18 | Learning and education |
| 4th | 18 – 24 | Detaching from parental home |
| 5th | 24 – 30 | Testing out life experiences |
| 6th | 30 – 36 | Coping with and establishing autonomous existence |
| 7th | 36 - 42 | Intense outward focus, relationships, partners |
| 8th | 42 – 48 | Transformation and rebirth; mid-life crisis |
| 9th | 48 – 54 | Formation of individual life philosophy |
| 10th | 54 – 60 | Authority, individuation, self-realisation |
| 11th | 60 – 66 | Freely chosen friends and relationships |
| 12th | 66 - 72 | Introversion, solitude |

**Figure 2. Life phases through the houses in Age Progression**

## Development of Age Point in aspect to ego planets

The mind, the emotional functions, and the body play instrumental roles in the development of the human personality interacting with his/her environment; and one of these is favored by the individual as the strongest and most preferred function for integration of the personality. As ego development proceeds, an individual may use: (1) the mind to make decisions as she faces life's problems; (2) a feeling based subjective faculty to choose between an alternative set of values to decide; or (3) his/her physical body's experience of protection and safety as a basis of attraction or repulsion to life events. One of these functions will have been well developed in an "average expected environment" and is used by the growing human to reliably navigate his/her world. His/her ego identity becomes consciously fused with one: the mental process, the emotional processes, or the body processes. The astrological psychology consultation assists with the choosing of the strongest of these three psychological functions as the basis of personality integration. And it so happens that, in the course of development, one of these chosen functions will synthesize the other two and additional psychological drives into a reliable method of coping with life's gains and losses.[xiii]

Planetary placements and aspects to the three ego planets symbolize the quality of mind (Sun), emotions (Moon) and body (Saturn). When each of these three ego planets is aspected by the AP, it will affect the inner life of the person and may challenge his/her functioning of the mind, emotions or physical body.

As the human being develops, these ego functions together with other planets—Mars, Venus, Mercury, Jupiter, Uranus, Neptune and Pluto—represent the psychological drives interacting in the arena of the environment of the twelve houses. The AP aspects these drives (planets) as it traverses the houses. For example, if one has developed his Sun ego planet and it is in the seventh house, a logical and an objective approach to problem-solving with relationships will most likely inform him on his attitude toward partnerships. When the AP is conjunct the natal Sun in the seventh house, then an energized and independent spirit will be infused in partnerships. It will be a turning point as significant commitments and relationships are made[xiv]. Usually this will occur for this person around age thirty-seven at the beginning of the house, a phase that Huber defines as "intense outward focus".[xv] If the natal planet Mars is opposed to the natal Sun then, as the AP travels through the 7th house, assertive or competitive mental energy will be expressed in partnerships, and may add aggressiveness to encounters.

## Developmental tasks and ego planet identification and beyond

As individuals continue to grow and develop throughout life, the chosen ego planet will remain a reliable basis for whatever environmental problem one meets. When the individual reaches psychological maturity, the deployment of ego energies is useful to environmental adaptation. But when the direction of life changes or a crisis occurs, in any life arena one can get stuck and not know how to proceed. For example, when one retires from active life, as the AP traverses the 12th house, isolation and introversion become developmental tasks.

Adjustment to this task, according to the psychosynthesis method, can call for a degree of disidentifying with the dominant ego function/planet. The consequence of this process means that one could deliberately diminish a reliable operating function of the psyche in the environment that had been used for dealing with life's problems during self-development. This apparent reversal may be disorienting and confusing, especially if one is not confident in self-esteem and cannot willfully adjust to the challenge of disengagement from the outer world. This dis-identifying process is similar to Jung's individuation process of becoming whole by reducing tension between opposites in the psyche. The process is clarified as the need for self-actualization as one matures. One makes a moral decision not to over-identify with one's dominant ego function, but to employ opposite functions as well in guiding the perception and decision-making process. These psychic developments beyond identification with the ego often usher in transpersonal experiences and raise consciousness to a very different world view from the one that we develop when we are in the process of maturing our ego identity.

## Dreams and Developmental Challenges

It is helpful and validating to discover through AP analysis that passages over sensitive areas in the horoscope can inform the individual of a way out of a dilemma. A problem or crisis encountered can be understood in the context of developmental life challenges posed by the AP progression. I believe it is a beginning, but not a complete answer. I believe that unconscious processing of complexes in the personal unconscious and the growth supporting aspects of the unconscious, as revealed in dreams, provide additional considerations for understanding one's life goal toward individuation. Our conscious mind with its denial, suppression and repression cannot alone access the deep pools within. Dreams inform the ego, based on triggers in everyday life experiences, of an additional context for life's problems. The unconscious formulates dreams based on triggers from daily life. Dreams loosen the complexes deep in the unconscious and change the ego identity as it is innervated and informed. This happens most of the time without our conscious awareness (see Figure 2.3 on page 71).

Dreams are not dreamed to be analyzed or understood, but an understanding of dreams tells us where the unconscious is already trying to alter the ego-image in the direction of health and individuation. Health and individuation, however, are not always aligned: what is "healthy for one dominant ego-image at a particular stage of life may be decidedly unhealthy for the nascent ego-image of the next stage of life".[xvi]

Furthermore, we could allow our conscious interpretation of AP progression and dreams to determine the outcomes of the transpersonal messages. Dreams come from the core of the individual, the Self. Through the psychic structure of the Self, the unconscious leads the ego, not the other way around. By leaving the insights from dreams out of an interpretation of age progression, astrologer and client could miss an opportunity to fill out the total picture. Of course, the unconscious speaks to us in many ways: not just through dreams, but also through poetry, visual arts, music, active imagination, meditation, contemplation, and other forms of experiences that invoke unconscious contents and the Self. But our focus here is on dreams, and here we stand on the threshold that leads to the "royal road to the unconscious".

Knowledge of one's dreams and techniques of amplification can provide personal solutions to life's problems, and a degree of comfort and validation when made conscious. By bringing the unconscious material of dreams into awareness, a broadening of perspective occurs that is specific to the journey of individuation as depicted by Huber's life phases. The personal challenges and solutions that are elicited through dream content analysis and their symbolic pertinence to the soul's growth cannot be overstated.

Roberto Assagioli, the founder of Psychosynthesis, did not fully agree with dream analysis as a method of personality integration:

> *"Although dreams do give access to the unconscious of the subject… [they] often only give access to one part of it—only one part of the unconscious is able or cares to express itself in dreams… in our practice we point out dream interpretation is only one of the techniques and not the chief one".*[xvii]

I prefer a Jungian interpretation of dreams in that they are capable of being understood in the context of triggers from daily life. Dreams display either personal or collective conflicts (i.e. complexes) within the individual, which they dramatize. I promote the cause that dreams have a direct correspondence with the temporal struggles within our individual psyches as we are on the path to self-realization, especially in the context of real life events and AP progression through the houses.

## The Meeting of Real Needs; Assagioli and Maslow on Transcendence

Assagioli believed, as did the great transpersonal psychologist Abraham Maslow, that there is a hierarchy of basic needs (See Figure 1.2 on page 42). Humans need a psychosynthesis that addresses basic reality needs for dealing with the difficulties of life and living. For example, someone with a substance use disorder that interferes with his holding a job and making a living could not approach divinity until the basic needs of sustaining a living have been satisfied. But once these physical and psychological needs are met, then the individual can be motivated to concurrently strive toward self-actualization,[xviii] which is a focus in this work.

In the model for recovery from addictions used by the self-help groups, Alcoholics Anonymous and Narcotics Anonymous, one of the mainstays is "surrendering to a higher power".[xix] Through submission one can have inner guidance peak experiences, *"direct revelation from God… and [these] revelations are seen as valid psychological events… which represent an awakening in the individual to the capacity for rapture, transcendence, self-realization and the aim of religion"*.[xx] Self-actualization can also be experienced through the revelations of one's dream work at the time when they correlate with AP aspects to sensitive points in the individual horoscope. The experience for the individual can be a realization that one is guided by a transpersonal power to experience acceptance and growth as revealed through ones' dream content.

Roberto Assagioli used concepts of the transpersonal self, spirituality and esoteric philosophy to a greater depth than Carl Jung. And this legacy is a wonderful complement to my dream analysis endeavors. When we reflect on our deficiency needs, on our "being needs", and how these needs are met, we can then become clearer about our life's choices—something both esoteric philosophy and psychosynthesis stress. Knowledge of one's dreams can provide the necessary understanding of the unconscious issues that are confronting the individual at a given time and elevate his/her sense of meaning beyond his/her ego attachments. With aging comes a decrease in body strength, a limiting of some body functions and a slowing of short-term memory access to the autobiographical memory bank; therefore, the developmental stage is set in the elder for working on spiritual goals. Also, emotionally-laden complexes loosen with aging, resulting in the possible occurrence of behavioral outbursts. These aspects of normal aging can have consequences that can alienate the person from himself and others leading to depression. That is one reason why the introverted process of dream analysis can provide a door to the unconscious in a manner that is self-revelatory, balancing these psychic energies, and giving meaning to life as one ages.

Assagioli's psychosynthesis sub-personality model stresses that solving our *needs* brings us closer to our real Self than following our *wants*. In his model, the aim is to recognize how sub-personalities distract us from becoming self-congruent by following our wants and desires.[xxi] Assagioli used Eastern methods akin to meditation and yoga, as well as Western Christian Mysticism, Hermeticism, Theosophy and Magic. These methods were employed in the service of self-actualization, which included a deep transformation in the individual learning to detach from his/her ego attachments. A vital method of meditation for Assagioli's practitioners is the use of dis-identification exercises. That is because at all stages of life we can over-identify with ego attachments that can interfere with revelations from the super-conscious, from the spiritual or transpersonal levels. An exercise such as "The Inner Guide" is a guided meditation that helps us to separate our wants from our needs, opening the pathway to the real Self.[xxii] This will be explained further in Chapter 3.

Maslow's hierarchy of needs will be discussed in Chapter 2. To support a client's meeting of his/her needs—physiological, safety, belonging/love, esteem—self-actualization leads to ego development and parallels what I believe Assagioli aims at in psychosynthesis (Figure 3 on page 10). The sub-personalities of clients demand a satisfaction of wants which provide a more divergent, distracting and illusionary path to spiritual development. Submitting to sub-personality wants does not lead to ego dis-identification, self-realization or self-actualization, but only knits the client's attachments to the ego. Ego attachments are good for individualization but, once a solid ego identity is formed and self esteem results, one can learn to transcend ego attachments to that identity and be congruent with spiritual realities like universal love (symbolized by Neptune), universal humanitarian values (symbolized by Uranus), and self-purification through supplication to the divine will (symbolized by Pluto).

Psychosynthesis methods use visualizations to help one enter different levels of consciousness. The visual image of a meadow is used to represent the edge of consciousness and is an amplification technique used to help one re-enter a dream,[xxiii] which in this author's examples comes from the transpersonal self.

Assagioli's egg model in Psychosynthesis depicts the junction where the field of awareness in the middle unconscious meets the transpersonal self (see purple vertical line in Figure 3), allowing for an exchange of information from different levels or boundaries in the psyche.

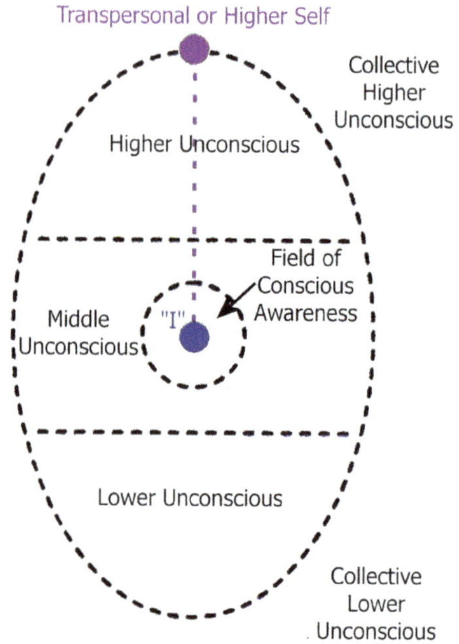


**Figure 3. Psychosynthesis Egg Diagram[xxiv]**

Assagioli's model is aligned to the concept presented by my work which asserts how an understanding of dreams can provide messages from the transpersonal self to the field of awareness in the individual.

## Huber and Erikson's Developmental Scheme

I use Huber and Erikson's developmental psychology models to provide a broader understanding of dream interpretation. Psychosynthesis methods for guided meditation and personality qualities needed to dis-identify with the ego attachments will be given to help to attain higher states of awareness and receptivity to Self contents (Chapter 2).

## Overview

The arguments that this work presents, cover the following:

1. Chapter 1 describes Huber's Life Clock method, as used in this presentation of AP progression correlated with dreams for all the planets in aspect to it, the houses involved, and other sensitive points. It also includes comparison of Huber's AP progression phases with Erikson's psychosocial tasks, which are invaluable tools in identification of dream work contexts. How the APs, as they traverse sensitive points of the chart, can give insight, validation and direction to one's life.
2. Chapter 2 expounds on aspects of astrological psychology that support ego development and the use of pychosynthesis and initiation into methods that transform consciousness. I describe the model of sub-personalities and its relationship to ego-integration. I clarify the roles of environment and heredity in achieving ego identity and increasing self-esteem. I address ways in which the transpersonal self can be revealed through dream work and lifestyle changes that can guide the individual toward a greater understanding and solution to life's problems and spiritual issues.
3. Chapter 3 includes a twofold approach to dream recovery: one in which incubation and amplification of dreams will utilize free association of symbols related to the dream content. How guided meditation can be used to further one's receptivity to dream content as it enters the field of awareness from the transpersonal Self. Dream recall, amplification and interpretation of the AP context will be covered.
4. AP progressions are correlated with dreams in the context of developmental challenges with volunteer subjects in Chapter 4. AP aspects to sensitive points are presented. The volunteers' dreams and insights are shared, and their dreams are presented according to their developmental sequence.
5. A summary of an Astrological Psychology consultation using dreams and developmental challenges to understand current problems is discussed in Chapter 5.

# Chapter 1. Huber's Life Clock

*"Knowing that the horoscope is such a measuring device or diagnostic instrument is invaluable in psychological practice. The trained eye can identify current problems and offer possible solutions. Not only does the knowledge save time but, with the help of age progression, a remedial program within time is possible."*

Bruno Huber in *Life Clock*

The understanding and use of the life clock implies first an awareness of the foundation principles of life, the timing of events in our lives and the execution of those events for ourselves and others. Western esotericism is defined for the initiated and the astrological psychology practitioner as first accepting the principle of correspondences[i]— "as above, so below," or what happens on the macrocosmic level with the planets, their movement around the zodiac belt, and their relationship to each other has relevance to my life on earth. There is a link between the macrocosm and the microcosm. By observing nature's cycles, rhythms and patterns as reflections of divine timing, we become aware of an objective movement in our lives, which reveals issues we must face and attend to that become pertinent at critical times.

*"A time to give birth and a time to die*
*A time to plant and a time to uproot what is planted*
*A time to kill and a time to heal*
*A time to tear down and a time to build up*
*A time to weep and a time to laugh*
*A time to mourn and a time to dance*
*A time to throw stones and a time to gather stones*
*A time to embrace and a time to shun embracing*
*A time to search and a time to give up as lost*
*A time to be silent and a time to speak*
*A time to love and a time to hate*
*A time for war and a time for peace."*

Ecclesiastes 3: 1-8

The life clock is a metaphor of the seasons of our lives in which we act, and we are self-aware of our execution. Humans have a capacity for self-reflection and an awareness of the meaning of their actions. There is a spring for setting our seed in its environment and nurturing it, summer for trimming and pruning of our growth, fall for reaping what we have sown and evaluating its quality, and winter for understanding the whole process of our cycle of life and preparing for our expiration.

During these times, we make psychological adjustments to the demands of that "season". In childhood and youth, we are physically growing and psychologically experiencing an awareness of ourselves as people. Then we are aware of our physical characteristics: are we a fast runner, can we play with other kids in a friendly manner, can we ride a bike? We reflect on our possessions and how we perceive our worth. We learn, love and belong to a family, express our creativity and are proud of our abilities. As we move into the summer of our lives, we work, and form partnerships that encounter the other with acceptance or rejection. Then, at mid-life, summer begins and we reflect on where we have been and where we are going; psychological adjustments are made, and we develop a philosophy with the realization that we are individuals trying to be authentic and assume authority for our own self-realization. In winter, we decline in physical strength, are aware of our loneliness, and may find a new orientation to life and death as we face our mortality.

The second principle for understanding the life clock is to learn how to change oneself and be receptive to these truths, first as a student and then as a teacher. The life clock is a measuring tool to apply to our own lives, to understand our tasks, our limits and our potentials. In this way, we become enlightened as to the governing principles of psychological growth for humans and humbled by the underlying guidance of the Divine in our lives, which is revealed through the AP movement in the life clock. This leads to a transmutation or rebirth in us as practitioners. These are additional criteria of esotericism, which tasks one to work on him/herself so that he/she has the knowledge and the temperament to provide guidance using this language.[ii]

Bruno Huber, in his work on the life clock, identified phases of life in a precise manner to illustrate the psychological and developmental tasks one must accomplish, as the AP goes through the twelve houses. He used this life clock model to transmit illuminations gained by observation and the message of the gestalt of the horoscope. This is the final step in esoteric astrology.[iii] These acts of communion and communication stress that when we work with our clients, we tune into their developmental phase, their awareness of it, and use this understanding as a point of departure for our consultation. We are not lecturing on theory and principles of esoteric astrological psychology. We must get to the point. The life clock presented by the Hubers through the process of AP progression is a metaphor for psychological growth through the life cycle and, as a form of esoteric astrology, it is made comprehensible to the client by analogy.

**What are the Houses?** The twelve astrological houses symbolize the stages of human involvement with environments.[iv] The horoscope shows the position of the planets in the houses at the time of birth and represents the human being as a subjective center in his proper value-position within the environment.[v] The houses constitute one of five elements in an astrological consultation: "In contrast to the unique core structure of the individual (aspects, planets and signs), the houses are an exterior, not a primary influential configuration reference. The house formation begins only with birth, and the individual deals with it his whole life."[vi] Figure 1.1 on page 16 shows the general meaning of the environment that each house contains.

## Age Point (AP) Progression in the Houses

The zodiac belt encircles our earth and is divided into twelve signs from Aries, Taurus, Gemini, Cancer, etc., through to Pisces. If we take a snapshot of the sky at the place and moment of birth, we get a picture of the planets in the zodiacal belt which corresponds to the natal chart. A similar division into twelve houses starts with the sign on the eastern horizon at the time of birth. Some of the natal chart's houses contain planets that give them special meaning. The houses are symbolic of the environment; the planets in houses represent the psychological drives that energize the houses. Some houses are empty and some are full. When a planet is positioned in a house, it represents drives associated with energies given to that arena of the environment and promotes action.

For Bruno and Louise Huber, the life clock reflects the movement of an AP through the twelve signs and houses of the zodiac in a given lifetime. As it moves, the AP highlights crises and opportunities in a psychologically developmental process. The AP contacts aspect patterns which are angular patterns among the planets, revealing personal, innate attitudes. Aspect patterns are composed of cardinal linear (multiple lines), quadrangular fixed (four sided), or triangular (three-sided) or mutable figures. Aspect patterns symbolize attitudes and unconscious motivation impacting behavior.[viii] These aspect patterns are innervated when contacted by AP progression through

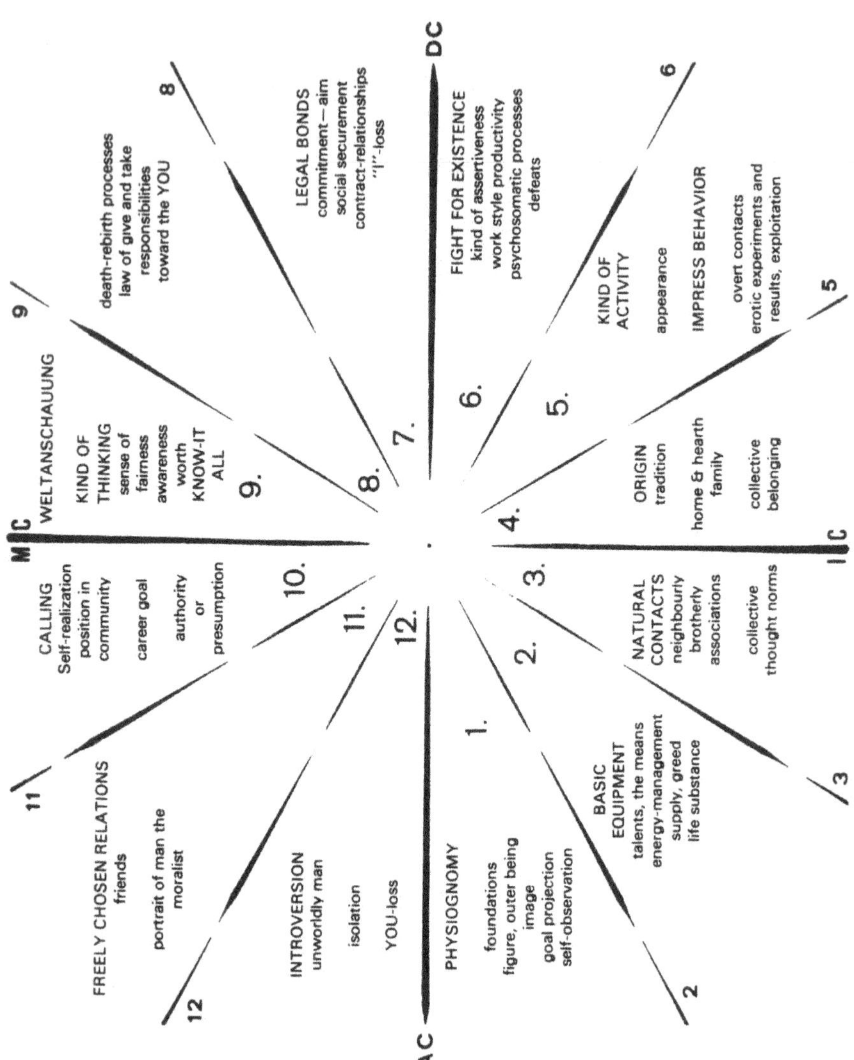


**Figure 1.1 Meaning of the Houses**[vii]

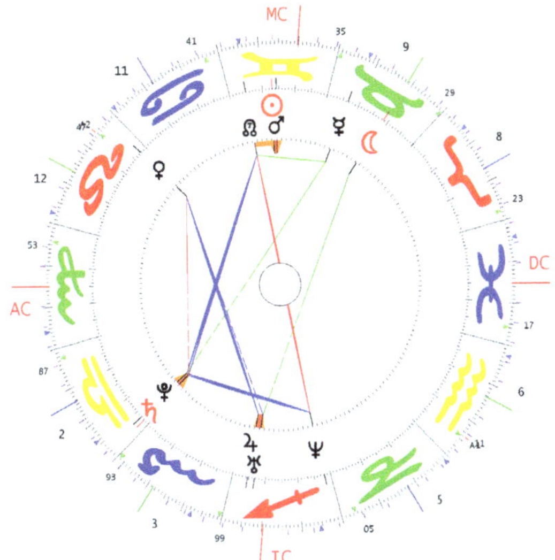


**Figure 2.1 Chart for the establishment of API(UK)**

the houses. Most horoscopes contain a combination of aspect patterns, e.g. triangular and linear as in Figure 2.1.

At birth, the AP starts at the Ascendant at the beginning of the first house. The AP takes six years to move through each of the twelve houses of the zodiac and one revolution spans 72 years; then it is back to the beginning of house 1 (see Figure 2 on page 4).[ix] The relationships of Age progression, sensitive points and aspect patterns in the natal chart, and the AP's movement through the twelve houses are the foci of my psycho-developmental approach to Astrological Psychology. Dreams are dreamt at critical times in the passage of the AP; therefore, we correlate the two in this work.

The houses define the external context that the individual will address as she strives to master life tasks. The psychological outlook the person brings at the time when the AP traverses a given house and sensitive points therein is the innovative contribution of Bruno and Louise Huber. They identified the seventy-two sub-life phases which define the developmental opportunities and crises one faces as the AP moves. For example, if the AP is in the third house when the individual is thirteen, she is in the sub phase of puberty, romanticism, idea formation. The outlook is going to be related to external opportunities for communication, learning and education. Since there are twelve houses, each one has a different outlook that determines the quality of psychological perspective and what the environment might offer.

**What is the empty center or core of the horoscope?** We do not exist in isolation in the world, there is a higher power which we say has a higher level of consciousness than the rest of humanity. It is God, or *"beings on other levels of consciousness that can have an effect on our progress on this earthly plane"*. There is a divine, trans-personal source of love and will that emanates from the somewhere we might call, the 'source of everything' (in the field[x]). Entities that exist on other levels of consciousness can assist us in grounding this trans-personal energy."[xi] The central core of the horoscope represents the divine source of everything. It is from this God energy that our human existence manifests and gives us form. These transpersonal qualities come from this represented center of the horoscope and divide into aspects and aspect patterns in the chart. So, the empty center is where guidance can come from the entities which communicate through dreams and lead us to higher states of consciousness. *"Higher states include having awareness of universal equality and love of everything that exists, possessing wisdom, joy in being, transcending duality in the world, having good will toward all, independence and power."* [xii]

The center core (Figure 3.1) of the horoscope although symbolic, is never drawn through in the erection of charts; it is always empty. Huber goes on to summarize that *"The reciprocal interactions among the central core (circle in the middle), the core energies or functioning organs (the planets), the signs as cosmic stimulators and modifiers, and the different arenas (houses), together make up the whole human being."* [xiii]

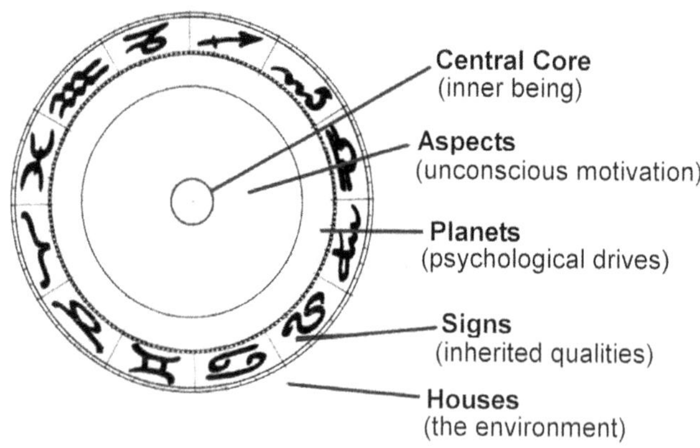


**Figure 3.1 Central core and levels of chart**

**What are the planets?** A planet symbolizes ability, a psychological force which we can apply in life. Each human being has ten such basic faculties that can be used to cope with all life situations. When the AP comes into contact with this psychological drive by aspect, the specific energy will be activated and brought into consciousness. Planets in houses have an effect on the specific environment that the house represents. For example, Mars in the first house has active and assertive drives expressed in the context of the persona, self-image and goal projection. See Figure 4.1 on page 20.

Each planet is represented by a glyph that has historically stood for the combinations the circle of spirit, cross of matter, and crescent of the moon. For example, Mercury is a combination of the crescent of the moon above the circle of spirit above the cross of matter (Figure 5.1 below.)

| Ego Planets | | Tool Planets | | Transpersonal Planets | |
|---|---|---|---|---|---|
| Sun | ☉ | Mercury | ☿ | Uranus | ♅ |
| Moon | ☽ | Venus | ♀ | Neptune | ♆ |
| Saturn | ♄ | Mars | ♂ | Pluto | ♇ |
| | | Jupiter | ♃ | | |

**Figure 5.1. The glyphs of the planets**

**What is the Nodal axis?** "The position of the moon node axis in the chart has considerable personal significance; an understanding of its meaning can give valuable insight into where we may be 'stuck' in our lives and what action may be taken in everyday situations for us to move on".[xv] The house placement and sign of the north node can give a hint to areas of possible growth and development. The south node's house placement and sign represent the past and the line of least resistance, where no growth takes place but just a repetition of the past. The nodes of the moon are not planets and therefore have no energy by themselves. The nodes are passive; they are acted upon by aspects from planets, AP progression, transits and progressions. Glyphs: north node ☊ south node ☋.[xvi]

The **Sun**. Represents the mentality of the human being; the quality or condition of self awareness. It represents the vital energies and has a directing function in relation to the planets. Its most important function is willful direction of energy. Potential energies: awakening, becoming yourself, contacting your essential nature, 'I know who I am.'

The **Moon**. Shows the emotional nature of man, his wish for contacts on all levels, his need for tenderness and understanding. As a reflecting principle, its central function is sensitive adaptation to life. Potential energies: intense emotional experience, greater need for contact with others, possibly childbirth.

**Mercury**. Enables us to assimilate our experiences mentally. It symbolizes our need for learning, gathering information and knowledge, and translates everything into words and concepts – communication. Potential energies: teaching learning, time of being heard, possibly a new job.

**Venus**. The aesthetic principle, always seeks balance and harmony in order to reach a condition of perfection. It is an introverted tool of selection in any assimilation process, the female libido. Potential energies: friendship, compromise, pleasure, having a good time, selectivity in relationships.

**Mars**. Expresses productive activity, the ability to convert energy into performance and work. Mars symbolizes the extraverted involvement and motion, the masculine libido. Potential energies: new strength, improved performance, courage, motivation to try new things.

**Jupiter**. Symbolizes the sense function with which we perceive the world: value consciousness, sensuous joy, capacity for judgment, perspective and fairness. Potential energies: time of expansion, forming own philosophy, personal growth.

**Saturn**. Corresponds to the physical, the sense of form, the need for order and demarcation that secure and protect life but also may make it more difficult. Saturn's symbolism suggests security and the wish for peace and comfort and also the status quo. Potential energies: Important lessons, achieving security, safety needs, building foundations.

**Uranus**. Creative intelligence, seeking new horizons in everything; the spirit of research and discovery; gaining security through technical and spiritual systems. Potential energies: unexpected events and changes, restlessness.

**Neptune**. Universal love, our highest love ideal; the ability to identify idealism; the will to help; social involvement. Potential energies: confusion, being in a fog, creative expression, spiritual awakening.

**Pluto**. Symbolizes the higher self, the spiritual will, the essential motivational forces which can transform the persona. Metamorphosis of personality. Potential energies: mutation, rebirth, deep changes in personality.

**Figure 4.1 The Planets' psychological meaning**[xiv]

**Age point progression and intensity curve in the houses:**
Each of the twelve houses is divided into three regions by an intensity curve (Figure 6.1 below):

1. the cusp or cardinal position to the balance point;
2. the middle area from balance point or fixed position to the low point;
3. the low point to the next house cusp area or mutable position.

Figure 6.1 depicts the level of energy intensity, high points and low points.

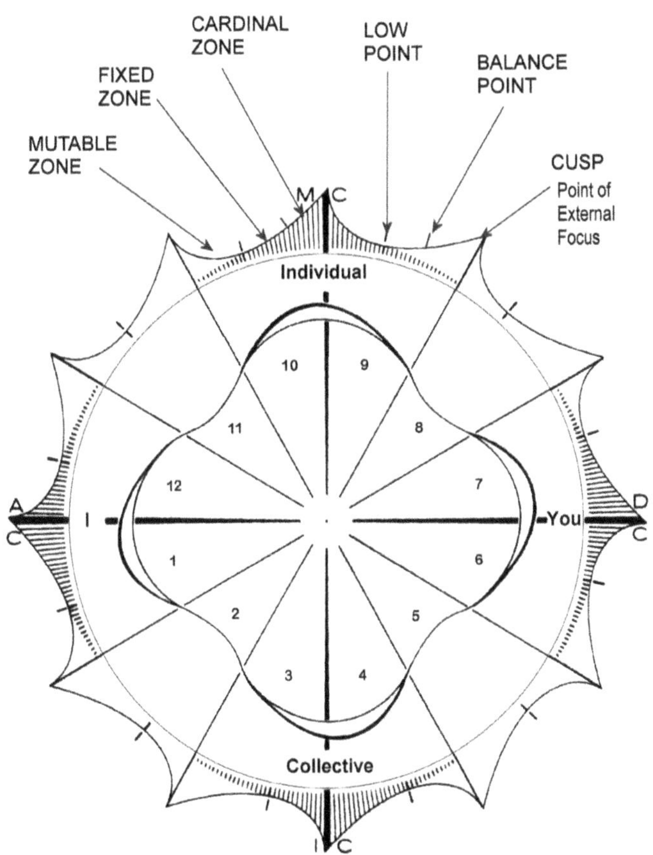


**Figure 6.1 The house intensity curve**

The strongest and weakest placements of AP progression in aspect to natal planets occur in the stressed area just before the cusp (beginning) of the next house, on the cusp, and on the low point. These represent different qualities in energy extension to the outer world:

- the cusp phase represents construction and action and expending energy to achieve external goals;
- the low point phase represents retrenchment, rest, turning inward through different ways according to the crosses: cardinal, fixed and mutable.[xvii]
- the stressed area in the mutable zone represents a pulling of energy from the rest of the planets so that they can satisfy environmental demands in two house areas often leading to compensations.

Developmental opportunities and crises appear when the AP is in angular relation to the planets (drives) that inhabit a house in the natal horoscope. Figure 7.1 shows the factors that are usually considered to be of most significance in Age Progression.

1. Crossing a house cusp and entering another house with a new psychological theme
2. Approaching a Low Point requiring a new orientation and change in consciousness
3. Conjunctions or oppositions with planets
4. Entering a new sign when the basic outlook and motivation may change
5. Passing through an empty space

**Figure 7.1 Important Factors in Age Progression**

Low Point and Cusp are the points we focused on in our Dream correspondence research (Points 1 and 2 in Figure 7.1). For our six volunteer subjects discussed in Chapter 4, the dream correlations were done when the AP progression positions were in conjunction and opposition aspect to natal planets at the cusp, low point, and stressed positions before the cusp of the houses.

## What are the signs?

The signs refer to the basic attitude, whatever the inner, central yearning is in the life. The sign indicates the inner striving and yearning, which is instinctual and may or may not be in agreement with the possibilities and challenges given by the environment or house placement.[xviii] Sometimes the sign on the cusp of a house does not match the external conditions and what is expected of us, as revealed in the house placement. Sometimes it does. Our dreams will have a flavor in content corresponding to the innate temperament (sign) and how it fits with external conditions (house).

If, at age 7, I dream of a huge man taking away my toys when the AP is in Scorpio on the cusp of the 2nd house, then my dream content may be about big people taking away my (toys) possessions, for example. The dream would be triggered by an external event giving the impression that something I own was threatened to be taken away by another. Since this second house has to do with my possessions, to be threatened by someone taking them away (a big person stealing them) is a trait of Scorpio, and is not congruent with the reality of holding onto possessions, which is symbolized by the second house.

Planets in signs are linked with inherited qualities and may run in families. When the AP passes through a sign it may take from three to twelve years depending on the size of the house. Regardless of whether one or more signs, or part of a sign, are contained within its cusps, the AP passes through a house every six years. We will focus on dreams

**Figure 8.1 Signs and their glyphs**

that occur at the time when the AP is in a particular sign, reflecting the basic attitude and yearning to which the content of the dreams refers.

For example, when the AP is in cardinal signs (Aries, Cancer, Libra, and Capricorn) initiative for new creative processes is strengthened. A new path is created and the motion is forward. One feels motivated, inspired and goal directed. When the AP moves through fixed signs (Taurus, Leo, Scorpio and Aquarius), the needs for consolidation and perseverance are highlighted. We resist and defend ourselves against any outside threat to that which we have created and try to put things in safe order. When the AP moves through mutable signs (Gemini, Virgo, Sagittarius, and Pisces), discrimination within existing circumstances is awakened. We are willing to change direction; and as we move back and forth, we vacillate.[xix] We fluctuate between opportunities and short and long term goals.

## Aspects of the Age Points to Planets

Aspects of the AP to the planets are depicted in Figure 9.1 opposite as it contacts them moving through the signs of the zodiac in the circle of time. When the AP is within 3 degrees of exactitude to a planet, it is said to be in conjunction and, when it is within 3 degrees of 180 degrees, it is in opposition. The influence of the AP on the planet can last from 4 to 6 weeks as it approaches exact conjunction or opposition, and issues related to it can reach consciousness from 3 months before to 2 months after the orb is passed; although it can be experienced for a longer time on both ends.

For example, if the planet is at 22 degrees of Sagittarius and the AP is at 19 degrees, it would be said to be approaching conjunction. A person might feel the experience of the aspect 6 weeks before the applying aspect of the AP makes an exact conjunction to the planet. If the planet is Venus, then the awareness and need for growth has a compromising and friendly quality. However, it also depends on the house the conjunction is positioned in; if it is the 3rd house, then the environment is related to the sphere of learning, communication and education. For example, a dream may occur in which the image of the subject is in communication with a professor, and there is focus on the pleasant aspects of religion. One should look to day-to-day life triggers of a dream that represents real issues, real people who might have sparked the image of a professor. If the AP is within a 3-degree orb of an opposition or 180 degrees, it is said to bring us an objective look at the energies of the planet. If the age point is within the orb of a conjunction, it can bring an awareness of the need for growth (Figure 9.1). In my experience, dreams are most important at times of conjunction and opposition to the AP: a conjunction, because the primary impression that is made will be experienced as an essentially psychological event and can readily show up in dreams; an opposition, because when the AP opposition to a natal planet occurs, a solution may present itself and be reinforced in dreams to correct the consequences of early impressions, or to overcome a faulty reaction.[xx]

It should be noted that we do not predict events with AP aspects, but we have an inner experience of them. The inner images we get in dreams coexist with these AP aspects. However, dreams can be precognitive and, if the AP is in opposition to a planet—say the Sun—the dream could make us aware that currently we cannot perform according our will, but anticipate a time in future in which our will could be fulfilled. Specific events that are connected to psychological processes may be triggered by a transit of a planet. Below is a diagram of the AP's effects on the planets which I shall be using in this work.[xxi] The red highlights what aspects will be used.

## Age Point and Planets

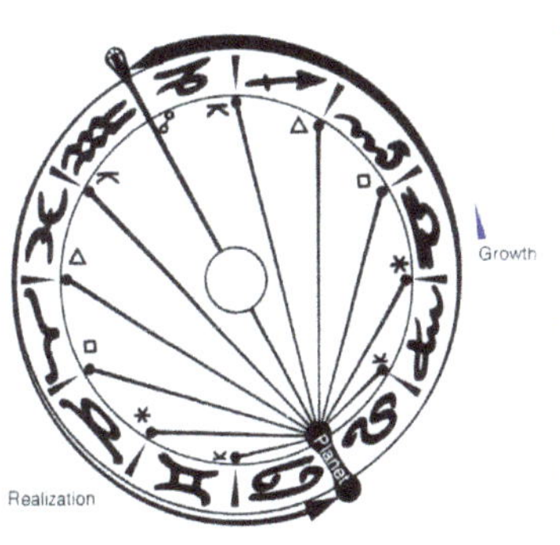


- 360° cycle is a cycle of growth
- Age Point conjunct planet - awareness of need for growth in issues related to planet
- Age Point aspecting planets - learning opportunities
- Age Point opposition planet - objective look at planetary energies

**Figure 9.1 Meaning of AP conjunct and opposed to a planet**[xxi]

## Erikson's developmental theory compared to Huber's

*a house by house interpretation*

The strength of a theory of development is more reliable when it has been repeated in other forms and other places. Huber's psycho-developmental theory of Age Progression throughout the life cycle is compatible to a similar theory put forward by the famous psychoanalytic theorist Erik Erikson.[xxiii] Below is a diagram of the models of Erikson's developmental stages compared to the phases of psychological development created by Bruno and Louise Huber:

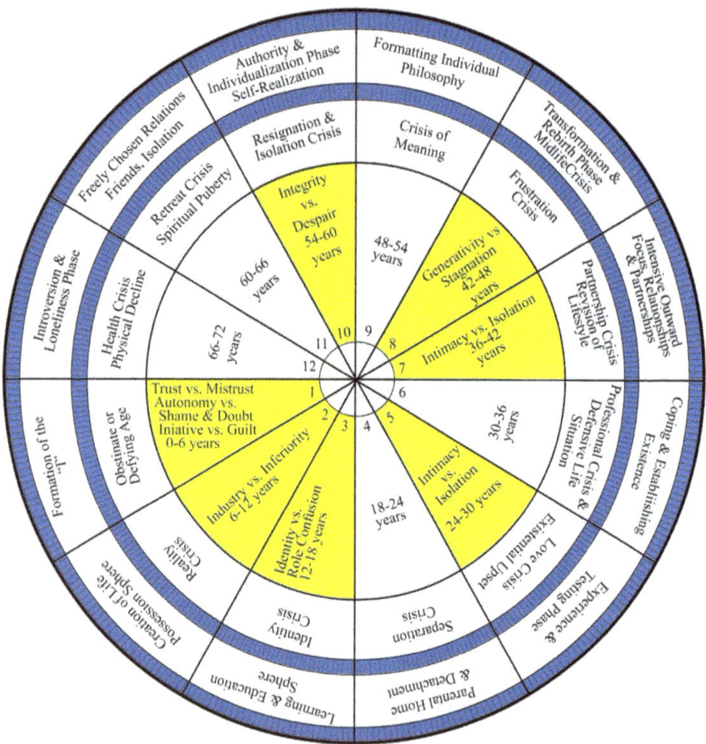


**Figure 10.1 Comparison of Huber and Erikson**[xxiv]

(See enlarged version on page 30)

The yellow area encompasses Erikson's eight stages of man, while the two white concentric circles surrounded by blue refer to Huber's phases of psychological development. Since Erikson was a medical doctor and psychiatrist and Huber was a psychologist, differences in focus are noted.

**House 1** of the horoscope is given a decidedly biological or physical emphasis by Erikson's 3 stages in this house:

*Trust vs. Mistrust*—oral stage of development in psychoanalytic theory, from ages 1-2 years. The child is developing her sucking and biting instincts. If the caretakers respond to her needs for food, nourishment and basic needs for security and love, she develops trust that her needs will be taken care of.

*Autonomy vs. Doubt*—anal stage of development in holding on and letting go of waste; the time for toilet training; from ages 2-4 years six months.

*Initiative vs. Guilt*—phallic stage in which the child is 'on the make' and trying to impress the mother or caretaker. He/she is interested in play and in creations he/she makes; from ages 4-7 years six months.[xxv] And she wants acknowledgement for her creations.

Compare this to Huber's formulation of the 'I' phase in the first 6 years, which encompasses house 1; the focus is psychological. Here he discerns that the preconscious and unconscious child is developing a sense of his/her differentiation from the environment but he/she is still fused with the caretaker/mother figure. In the last part of this phase, the child begins to awaken to a sense of others and may begin the need to identify with the caretakers.[xxvi] This house range of ages is from 0-6 years.

**House 2**: Stage IV is called by Erikson *Industry vs. Inferiority*,[xxvii] because developmentally this is when imitation of others builds the child's sense of self-image through assimilation. The developing ego of the child has completed differentiation between itself and the environment. The child continues to identify with others in his environment, especially peers. The first inkling of vocational interests emerges at the end of this phase. Erikson calls this stage the latency stage, which for him goes from ages 6-12, pre-puberty. Huber's psychological process involves a creation and holding on to personal possessions or talents assimilated from others that leads to a sense of self-worth. Huber calls this phase the creation of life and possession sphere.

In **House 3**, we observe that Erikson called Stage V *Identity vs. Role Confusion*;[xxviii] this is when the child begins to develop a sexual identity and attachments to vocational interests. In America, where there is usually a 'moratorium on life' due to the cultural value of freedom of choice of an identity, there is experimentation here, and a tentativeness in decision-making regarding what one's major identity may be.[xxix] Huber marks an identity crisis at about age 15-16. In the mutable third house, there is an age-appropriate vacillation of interests in identity and vocation. The range of ages for this house is from age 12-18, and this phase is referred to as the learning and educational sphere by Huber.

**Houses 4 – 7**: Erikson's Stage VI is called *Intimacy vs. Isolation.*[xxx] I correlate this developmental experience of maturing youth with the 5th and 7th houses in Figure 10 in Huber's model. Erikson's *Intimacy vs. Isolation* stage corresponds loosely with phases in Huber's 5th (ages 24-30) and 7th houses (ages 36- 42).

Huber describes the age range from 18-42 as a time of many developmental crises in his model. There is a need to leave the parental nest when the AP reaches the 4th house, which Huber linked with the parental home and detachment (ages 18-24); needs for relationship expression and self-promotion are themes of the 5th house, covering the experience and testing phases (ages 24-30); the 6th house involves the need for survival, with application of one's identity to earning a living, thereby coping with and establishing existence (ages 30-36); and the need for give and take in equal relationships with an intimate partner in the 7th house of intense outward focus on relationships and partnerships (ages 36-42).

In the Erikson model of the intimacy vs. isolation stage, reference is made to heterogeneous relationships. Here, Erikson is clearly out of date because he identifies intimacy with mutual orgasm achievement between a man and a woman. We recognize now that intimacy realizations can occur between same sex couples. It seems valid to include work in this stage of intimacy vs. isolation, because of Erikson's dictum of the need to 'work and love' at this time. Huber states that, following intensive outward focus in relationships and partnerships, the individual starts to have inklings of his/her mortality which lend themselves to reflection and changes in values related to self-care.[xxxi]

**House 8** reflects Erikson's Stage VII, *Generativity vs. Stagnation*, which leads to mid-life crisis and rebirth experiences, as one biologically feels a decline in physical energy, an urge to consolidate creative works, and think about lasting and enduring legacies (children or permanent works). Huber defines the psychological crisis of this 8th house as creating extreme frustration, due to needing to develop a new orientation to marriage, family and profession.[xxxii] For the Hubers, this is the mid-life crisis phase of transformation and rebirth. The age range for this house is 42-48.

**House 9** is the Hubers' phase of formulating an individual philosophy, described as a time of a crisis in meaning, spanning across ages 48-54. It can be assumed that part of *Generativity* for Erikson is the creation of a set of ethical values which would carry one to the end of life, but he is not as explicit as Huber about that issue.

**House 10** begins for Erikson with the ability to have *Integrity.* Because of declining energy, the impending loss of occupational identity in retirement, the onset of illness associated with aging, and other losses that come with final life issues. Ego integration involves the readiness to defend the dignity of his/her own lifestyle against all economic and physical threats. *Despair* represents the feeling that time is too short for the attempt to start another life, and it can manifest as fear of death.[xxxiii] Huber has identified this house with self-realization and individuation, both of which require a sense of wholeness and integrity in the face of threats and entitle one to the authority that comes with wisdom. It is 'the moment of truth', because isolation and resignation await the person who does not solve spiritual issues and ego integration, and fails to welcome a sense of tuning into his/her inner self. This is the peak of accomplishment, but outer rewards mean less at this phase.[xxxiv] The age range for this house is 54-60 years.

**Houses 11 and 12** extend Erikson's *Integrity vs. Despair* life task. For Huber, this phase includes the opportunity for freely chosen relationships and friendships, as we enter the isolation sphere by retiring from public life (11th house). Whether we deal with a reduction in personal striving or hold on to a persona we have built up, the resulting consequences will involve a change in ego-identity during these years. As we experience the sphere of introversion and loneliness, we may incur health crises and isolation during this 12th house passage of the AP. The range of ages 60-72 is appropriate here.

Although there is not a one-to-one correspondence between these two developmental theories, both approaches are closely related to each other. So when the AP progresses through the 12 houses, there are crises and opportunities for the individual to experience, especially at the beginning of houses and at low point positions contacted by AP transits through the twelve houses (see Figure 10.1, page 26).

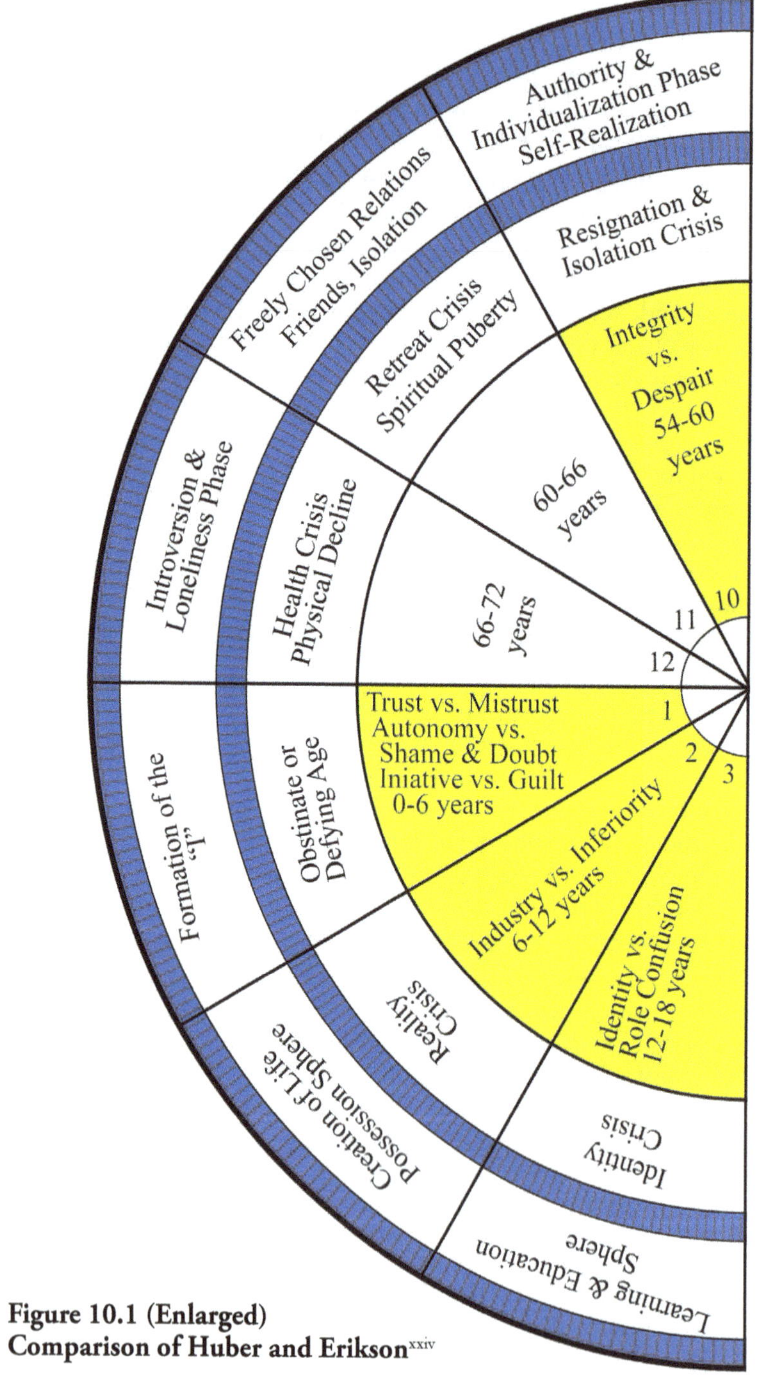


**Figure 10.1 (Enlarged)**
**Comparison of Huber and Erikson**[xxiv]

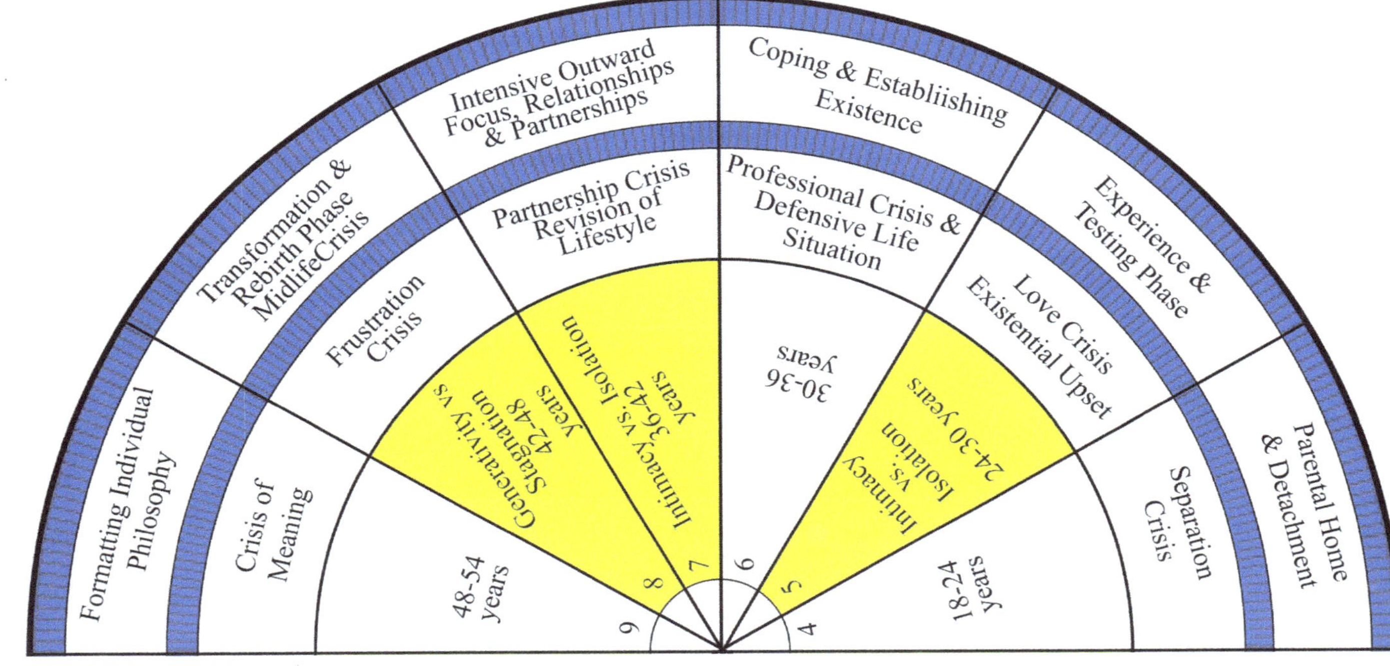
Formatting Individual Philosophy
Transformation & Rebirth Phase MidlifeCrisis
Intensive Outward Focus, Relationships & Partnerships
Coping & Establiishing Existence
Experience & Testing Phase
Parental Home & Detachment
Crisis of Meaning
Frustration Crisis
Partnership Crisis Revision of Lifestyle
Professional Crisis & Defensive Life Situation
Love Crisis Existential Upset
Separation Crisis
48-54 years
Generativity vs Stagnation 42-48 years
Intimacy vs. Isolation 36-42 years
30-36 years
Intimacy vs. Isolation 24-30 years
18-24 years
9
8
7
6
5
4

## Putting it all together - example dream at age 24

| Considerations for analysis of AP | Example | Interpretation | Dream and date/ Daily events log |
|---|---|---|---|
| **Date of AP aspect/age** | June 1973 | Age 24 | June 1973 |
| **House that AP is in?** | 5th house: experience and testing phase. Partnerships; Professional existence.[xxxv] | Travel and developing a definite commitment to professional life and love is emphasized. Going out in the world to take risks and test his identity is happening now. | **Dream:** John was standing on the edge of a cliff with Mother on his back; He could not jump the chasm before him with Mother on his back. He put Mother down on the one side and jumped across to the other side alone.<br>**Daily events:** He was about to leave for an assignment with the American Peace Corps in Oman. He would be teaching English as a foreign language to Arabs. He would be gone for 2 years. He was compelled to leave home and strike out on his own. |
| **Planet AP aspects?** | AP conjunction with Node | Aware of the need for his growth to take the opportunity to experiment with his identity as a teacher in a foreign land. | |
| **AP at cusp or low point?** | AP at cusp | Construction and action and spending energy to achieve external goals of leaving home for professional life. | |

| **AP in what sign –house correspondence ?** | AP in Taurus a fixed sign | Consolidation, and perseverance of his decision to join the Peace Corps is highlighted. John resists and defends himself against parent's recommendation for him to stay in the USA. He moves with determination toward this goal and will not be deterred. | |
|---|---|---|---|
| **AP to aspect figure formed?: linear, quadrangular or triangular.** | AP extends linear aspect figure and emphasizes movement | Motivated to follow his will and to attain goals and ambitions for an extensive exposure to the real world. | |
| **Natal Transits** | Transiting Neptune t in 12th house square Saturn n in 9th house; Transiting Saturn t in 7th house opposes Venus n in 1st house. | Moods and view of the world changes in a psychological structure that had been established. To serve demands of this phase some sacrifice of money and possessions as a volunteer. A crisis and testing of relationships as he leaves home for two years. | |

The above dream was experienced in June of 1973 by the author and when it is paired with AP progression in the houses and aspects to planets, a powerful interpretation can be discerned about developmental challenges and opportunities. We do not deal with the dream alone but in the context of what is happening in daily life, which is what usually triggers a specific dream.

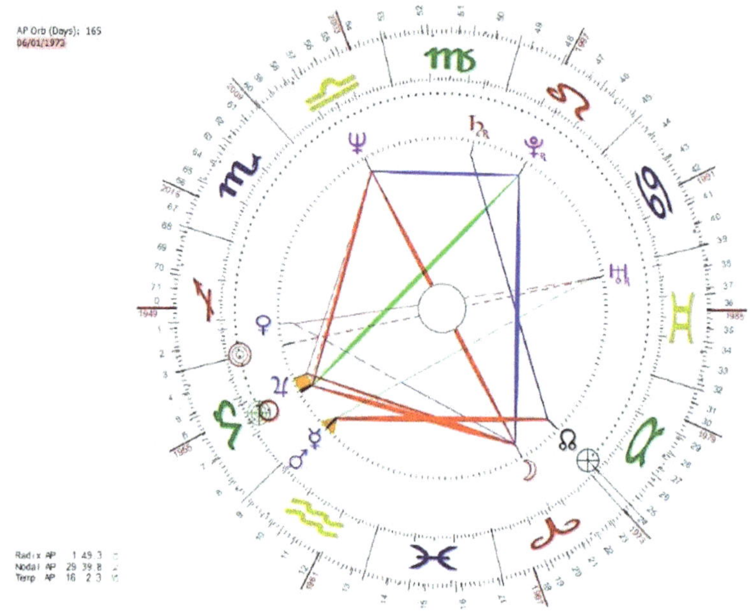


**Figure 11.1 John's Chart showing AP at 1st June 1973**

*Cross hairs show position of natal AP in Taurus.*

**What comes next**

Dream analysis with volunteers is covered in more detail in Chapter 4, but before then we consider how to work with dreams in Chapter 3. But first, in order to really make the most of dream analysis, the ego must have a firm foundation in reality, and in Chapter 2 we highlight how to support identification and integration of ego strengths in the personality, in the face of some adverse circumstances in life.

# Chapter 2. Life Tasks and Going Beyond

## Initiation into Higher States of Consciousness

*"From the earliest times there have always been human beings who have claimed that they experience states of consciousness that are vastly different in terms of quality, intensity and effect from those that normally cast their light and shadow on the screen of human awareness. But they make a broader claim: that these states of consciousness result from reaching, or involuntarily being brought into contact with a plane or sphere of reality which is 'above and beyond' those normally regarded as real"* [i]

Roberto Assagioli in *Transpersonal Development*

### Accomplishing Life Tasks and Ego Development

Clients who present with mental health problems and who are fortunate to experience clinical guidelines for treatment of mental health problems such as post traumatic stress disorder (PTSD) and bipolar disorder, receive medications and psychotherapy as first line treatments. Research shows that the treatment efficacy for remission of symptoms of combat related PTSD has a rate of about 70% but the clients still meet the criteria for PTSD;[ii] for chronic bipolar diagnosis the medication of lithium is effective for maintenance plus psychotherapy to prevent relapse.[iii] These clients rarely present themselves to my psychotherapy or astrological psychology consultations with questions about paranormal experiences or spiritual problems. They leave these problems to their pastor, priest, rabbi or mullah; at times, they quietly endure them. But clients who have a mental health diagnosis like chronic post-traumatic stress or bipolar disorder can succumb to the illusion that merely by identifying synchronistic events in their daily life, dreams and/or uncanny dissociative states of consciousness that they are having genuine spiritually uplifting experiences. The opposite is the case. Roberto Assagioli has made clear that sufficient psychic maturity is necessary to allow for the latent transpersonal dimension in the individual to be awakened. In a manic ego state, clients may cite epiphanies in which they think they experience extreme mental clarity; that is why they do not like the sedative effects of medication. But it is an illusion that they are anywhere near a spiritual experience because they must achieve psychosynthesis of the ego before spiritual development can occur.[iv]

Those with chronic post-traumatic stress disorder (PTSD) can be in extreme states of anxiety in which they are obsessed with wanting the symptoms of their intrusive thoughts and anxiety to go away. I have often met resistance in clients with PTSD who think marijuana meets a need for self-actualization. For these clients smoking marijuana in addition to taking medication can create a 'high' and this temporarily relieves but does not extinguish symptoms. By taking marijuana or illicit drugs, they miss the opportunities of down-regulating their central nervous system through interventions that require an active effort. They also do not work on the ego development necessary to function adaptively according to psychosynthesis principles. Instead, the experiences of these clients which seem to be spiritual or transcendent, without proper ego integration and psychosynthesis, are illusory and reflect the inflation of an unintegrated ego.

I mention these two diagnostic categories of clients from my psychotherapy practice as examples of distorted spiritual development, because they very commonly indulge in the recreational use of drugs, marijuana and alcohol. Many people think these drugs are agents of true spiritual experiences. Ego development and integration for clients is a question of whether they are motivated to work on their needs in therapy, not just what they want. The issue is whether a quick relief with street drugs is indicated vs. marshalling motivation to meet their needs via a mature adaptation in society.

For the bipolar client, taking the prescribed medication will stabilize their moods but may blunt their mental highs. Yet that may be just what they *need*. Whether they take medication or not, it is difficult to convince clients to try meeting their *needs* for ego development rather than just satisfying what they *want*.

With the client who wants an astrological consultation, assessment of how she relates to the meeting of her *wants* vs. her *needs* requires my discernment, too, in order to determine which distortions of wants caused by a sub-personality influence her behavior and prevent healthy ego psychosynthesis.

A psychotherapist and a consultant in astrological psychology have many interventions in common. However, in astrological psychology consultations, it is beyond the scope of practice to make a diagnosis. The common denominator for both psychotherapist and consultant is to be able to recognize true potential for transpersonal experiences in clients vs. those who just have delusions of grandeur.

The narcissistically wounded and bipolar clients may find that their delusions about being special or having a mission ordained by a higher power become dulled through focus by the therapist, who redirects them to what they need instead of indulging their illusions. And that work is boring, and requires their systematic confrontation with developmental challenges. Their illusions of having an already developed ego and possessing 'insights' into spirituality are often explained to them in popular literature as 'possessions' by entities.[v] These ego states, as I call them, can convince individuals that they are operating in a new stable identity but, No, this is a 'sub-personality' for Huber and Assagioli.[vi]

For those coming to an astrological consultation, integration of the personality and receptivity to spiritual experience can unfold only with psychosynthesis, as the sub-personalities lessen their influence. Those clients can become aware, with a therapist's or a consultant's prompting, of the existence of their sub-personalities and learn to decrease their power. But work on developing ego integration is not within the scope of practice of an astrological consultant. She can refer clients to psychotherapists, who can work on these issues if a client is receptive. This is especially pertinent when a client's behavior leads to distortions of reality and maladaptive behavior. Likewise, many clients who have human-caused PTSD experience negative emotional ego states in which they want to pull away from relationships and 'isolate' to lessen the intensity of intrusive thoughts, depressing emotions and/or anxiety symptoms. Some have a dissociative identity disorder, in which an ego state takes control of their ego identity, triggered by symbolic events that remind them of the original trauma. These clients can be helped to endure their suffering with the discerning eye of a psychotherapist who knows what is real development vs. what is fake.

Unconscious inflation of the ego through identification with a deity leads to grandiosity, as in bipolar illness. The immediate desire to lessen the anxiety symptoms of PTSD by social withdrawal or taking a hit on a cannabis joint distorts their *needs*. I do not believe in damping down or refuting a client's need for a relationship with the divine, or in passively watching clients suffer with anxiety symptoms. But when psychotherapy clients convince themselves that they can cope with their symptoms by identifying with their inflated ego or lessening anxiety symptoms by using a drug, or by socially isolating, that is where I use gentle therapeutic confrontation. Because when they avoid the work of symptom reduction, clients usually regress to maladaptive behaviors, which are self-defeating and do nothing to address the underlying illness.

The same can be true of people coming for an astrological psychology consultation; they may yearn for satisfaction of their desires by possessing a 'special relationship' with a partner, based on what a sub-personality wants. For example, a consultation can occur with a person who has a strongly developed Moon ego planet. To secure her love and the sympathy of others, she may develop a 'rescue complex'. This process results in her taking care of others to the detriment of meeting her own needs for autonomy. She may succumb to the illusion that she has met her needs for belonging but in fact has only wanted to be reassured that she would be loved and accepted. This pattern of behavior can defeat her need for security when she opens herself up for emotional rejection by being so dependent on others for love.

Special relationships are more illusory than real. It is a fallacy to think that by meeting their wants through sub-personality identification they are achieving the ego integration given priority by Huber and Assagioli's psychosynthesis. True spiritual development cannot occur until there is integration of the ego, involving identification of the strongest of the ego planets in astrological psychology terms and maturational development. I believe that when one recognizes that the client's developmental task is to increase her self-esteem based on challenges to ego integration, the astrological consultant can make a referral to a psychotherapist. Building and sustaining healthy ego integration is not static, and the process can be wounded by life's losses and the individual's interpretation of them. Self-confidence needs continual work, in my view, and the discipline to know how to combat negative self-talk is the domain of the psychotherapist.

My task in psychotherapy is to "teach clients to recognize a 'mystic' sub-personality as a defense mechanism and potential distortion of a clear connection to the Self."[vii] Clients are not to blame for trying to adapt to stress by taking refuge in defenses or believing that by doing what they want, they will satisfy their needs. Usually a passion or desire to achieve a certain state or goal is what motivates the client's sub-personality to manifest itself. Their egos want to 'possess' that state of consciousness which they believe finally satisfies the passions and desires feeding their ego. But, in the end, giving energy to passions and desires just increases their illusions, hurts self-esteem and security, and their real needs for love and belonging. It is a task of the psychotherapist to help clients recognize their need to align their egos with what they can realistically accomplish in the real world.

Helping clients to distinguish between the meeting of their *needs* rather than their *wants* requires discrimination to assist them on the road to recovery. The task is not to eliminate distortions permanently but to lessen them, so that reality testing, occupational work and adaptive social relationship functioning can occur. Once done, they can put off gratification of their wants and redirect their egos, so that they become subservient to their reality needs. This has the effect of supporting their sense of belonging, safety and self esteem. When they fail to do this, they mistake the sub-conscious for super-conscious, thereby missing the opportunity for even development of healthy integration of their egos into the Self, and a modicum level of social functioning.

In my 35 years as a psychotherapist and astrologer, I have learned that if clients can master and accept the progress they make in dealing with the crises relevant to the developmental task that accounts for the reason why they needed therapy, they will greatly improve their mental health. We can then terminate our sessions and speak of 'goals met by mutual agreement.' Then we can say that they have achieved psychosynthesis at a basic level with relatively healthy functioning.

However, for as many times as success announces itself in psychotherapy, so does failure. Even as I am motivated to help clients understand the states of consciousness that seem to interfere with their expected life goals, often they are not motivated to focus on giving their energy to the task at hand. The stubborn temptation to gratify *wants* obscures any real effort toward a mentally healthy outcome. I don't congratulate myself in these cases, because psychotherapy requires an effort of mutual application and discovery. So the two goals of (1) resolution of developmental crises and (2) normalization for the client of regressive states of consciousness are grist for the mill for what clients need from me as a therapist or consultant.

## Maslow's Hierarchy of Needs and Astrological Psychology's Ego Planets

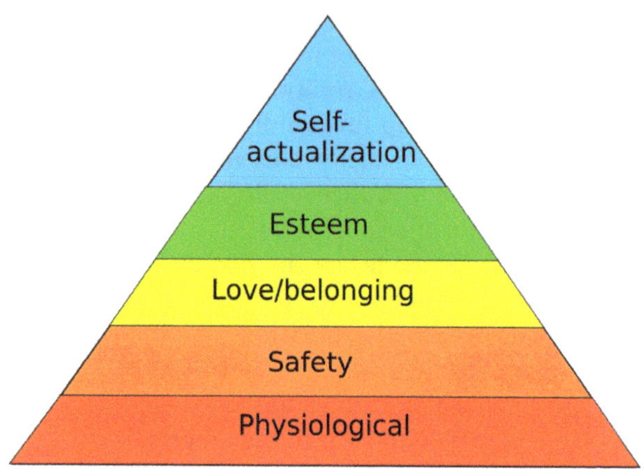


**Figure 1.2 Maslow's Hierarchy of Needs**

Clients may be motivated to face up to their basic needs both in therapy and in astrological consultation, instead of gratification of fantasies, wants or desires. To accomplish this, their ego needs must be recognized and supported by the therapist or consultant. First, there is the physical need for safety and security, which is achieved by building trust. There is a correlation between Maslow's hierarchy of needs and astrological psychology's ego planets. On the first two bars of Maslow's pyramid are physiological needs and safety (See Figure 1.2). These refer to nourishment and growth in the first four years of life, where 70% of development is physical. A parallel situation for the client in psychotherapy or astrological consultation relates to the provision of a secure framework in the client-consultant relationship where confidentiality, privacy and relative anonymity are the social norm.[viii]

This physiological bar correlates with the genetic endowment of the child and relies to a great degree on the 'average expected environment,' based on the early parenting on which the fulfillment of her/his hereditary endowment depends. The connection with astrological psychology is the correlation of the client's psychological drive for security and safety with the planet Saturn's horoscope placement. Saturn's placement and aspects are symbolized by the daily routines leading to safety and security of the child initiated by the mother. Saturn's patterns and aspects are identified in the natal horoscope and represented by the Mother's caretaking of the child. The Mother makes sure the child is fed, comfortable as to warmth or cold, clean and hygienically cared for, and established in the routines of the sleep-wake cycle. Thus, Saturn's quality in the horoscope can yield a great deal of information about the nature of the relationship between Mother and child, and form the structure of safety and security of physical functioning relating to Maslow's physiological and safety needs. In the astrological psychology interventions, the consultant provides safety and security for the client, a Saturn role, as a nurturer in this relationship. He provides consistency, structure based on the client's needs, and routine care for his client based on set appointment times. The office décor meets her needs for comfort, a nurturing environment, and relative security.

The second ego need is to be loved and have a sense of belonging. The love/belonging bar on the Maslow pyramid (Figure 1.2) correlates to the Moon in astrological psychology. This is the drive to contact others for the purpose of getting sympathetic love and emotional connection. Good emotional development means the child can reach out with trust to others, expecting a return of love and understanding. The Moon with its aspects and placement in the natal horoscope reveals the subjective point of view of the child as to how his emotional needs are met/not met. In an astrological psychology consultation, as in therapy, application of Carl Rogers' concept of 'unconditional regard,' given by the consultant to the client, must convey empathy and understanding, not judgment.[ix] In this way, we allow the spontaneous inner child in the client to contact the therapist.

The third ego need is correlated with the self esteem and self-actualization bars on the Maslow pyramid (Figure 1.2), and is symbolized by the Sun in astrological psychology. Qualities of the Sun refer to the psychological drive for thinking, conceptualization, and willing, which eventually can bring about self-realization and give a sense of purpose to the individual, once basic needs are met. Assessment of Sun principles by the therapist, can help determine whether the client has clear thinking, good problem solving capacity, and the potential to awaken the strongest ego planet. The astrological psychology consultant sets goals that align with the client's strengths, not his/her own. Therefore, at the beginning of a consultation, one must ask why the person is seeking consultation and try to focus on 'the presenting request' during the session, using the chart inferences to direct the flow of communication. A respect for the independence of the client is paramount to a good consultation. For the therapist, aligning with the presenting problem of the client is the initial goal of treatment. When the client suffers from a negative feeling or ego state in a consultation, the astrologer does not 'rescue' her from her struggles but, using empathy and applying active listening skills, is gently supportive as she works through her struggles.[x]

## The Matrix of good ego development

The mother or caretaker provides the safety, security and nourishment of the young child, and the child reaches out to contact others for love and a sense of belonging. When these contacts are reciprocated, her self-confidence builds, making her feel good about meeting her security needs. Saturn provides for the day-to-day supportive tasks that help the child build a healthy, strong body. The Moon provides a healthy reaching out to others in which one expects a return of love. The Sun builds up self-esteem as the child takes risks with a view to achieving her goals, developing the basis for pride, autonomy and self-awareness.

In astrological psychology, this epigenetic development of the human being will occur successfully when life tasks can be met by healthy development of one of the three ego planets. The ego planets, which Huber identified as Saturn, Moon and Sun, may have placements and aspects in the natal horoscope which yield valuable information as to the potential for the successful completion of life tasks. To review the following correlates with Maslow's hierarchy of needs:

- for physiological, safety needs, I correlate with Saturn
- for love needs, I correlate with the Moon
- for self-esteem needs, I correlate with the Sun

Information on the quality of the ego planets as they relate to the meeting of basic needs is determined by the exact birth time, place and date of the individual, and this data is calculated on a computer by the astrological psychology consultant to put up the natal horoscope. Assessment of the strongest ego planet is determined by its placement in the house system and its planetary aspects. Ego growth and development through identification and development of the strongest ego planet must be accomplished if personality integration is to be met. Are the will and thinking (Sun) determined to guide the individual through life as a thinking type? Are the body (Saturn), presentation of appearance and rituals of a physical nature the features that secure the personality through sensation and the nature of reality? Do the emotions (Moon) and their value judgments determine which of two alternatives subjectively feels right when making decisions?

In my practice, both as astrological consultant and therapist, many of my clients are confused by distortions of their ego needs, which hinder their awareness of the strongest ego planet or psychic faculty that will provide consistent behavior and choices. They can be distracted by their wants in an environment that may not support good development. Their sub-personalities take over, creating an inauthentic self. Whether a client is in psychotherapy or an astrological consultation, the goals are the same. Huber was wise to recognize the priority of ego integration and development before the achievement of higher levels of consciousness. Regression to meet desires, passions or wants on a continual basis, hinders our awareness of higher consciousness attainment. That is because these behavior patterns cannot be sustained and are not stable enough to lead to a good level of self-esteem that will allow for receptivity to the more transcendent vibrations of universal love (Neptune), universal humanitarian improvement (Uranus), and transmutation of the ego (Pluto). So, it is vitally important for me to identify and support the predominant ego function that guides the personality toward achieving confidence and building self esteem through its application in the real world.

## Archetypes, Ego Planets and the goal of Integration

Archetypes are thought to be aspects of the constitutional framework of inherited traits that predispose a child to be attracted to one of the three paths that are necessary for healthy ego development. The archetypes that reflect the ego needs of the child in astrological psychology are the following:

**The Mother**: physiological development and nurturance in a secure and safe relationship (as reflected by Saturn); this is illustrated in Figure 1.2 on the two lower bars.

**The Moon**: contact and sense of belonging (as reflected by Moon); this is illustrated in Figure 1.2 in the third bar from the bottom.

**The Father**: esteem and self-actualization (as reflected by Sun); this is illustrated in the two top bars in Figure 1.2.

The top bar, self-actualization, can lead to a transpersonal state of consciousness and depends on the previous levels' needs being met for it to be awakened.

It is necessary for a developing individual to identify with one of these ego symbols to facilitate integration of personality and become an effective agent in the world.[xi] This is a process that involves mature development, including identity formation, loving and working in the world.[xii] *'There is a special method of illustrating which of the ego planets is in the strongest position and thereby describes the perspective from which our self-awareness functions.'* The discovery of a strongest ego planet or archetype can be assisted by a client consultation with an astrological psychology counselor. Astrological psychology supports the concept that we build on our ego strengths through our awareness of them and how they adapt to environmental pressures or lack thereof. Then we apply our efforts to integrate our personality by application of the body, the emotions or the mind as faculties bringing a consistent method of understanding and working onto our place in the world. This is an unconscious process for some, conscious for others, facilitated by an astrological consultation and the awareness of the individual concerned. Integration through identification of the strongest ego planet or archetype is the most common type of goal setting, and is the focus of psychotherapy as well as astrological consultation.

Self-actualization may be achieved by my clients once they reach awareness and integration of the strongest ego planet or, as Jung called it, the dominant psychic function: thinking, feeling, sensation or intuition.[xiii] This confidence in their way of dealing with the world, reflected in the strongest ego planet, then becomes a point of departure which can increase a client's sensitivity to the transcendental energies of the planets Uranus, Neptune and Pluto. The irony is that once ego integration has been achieved, then one can begin the process of dis-identifying with the ego so that receptivity to higher states leading to self-actualization can begin.

## Heredity and the Environment together impact Behavior

Studies of monozygotic twins have supported the scientific view that genetics play a significant role in temperament.

> *"Behavioral genetics studies heritability of behavioral traits, and it overlaps with genetics, psychology, and ethnology (the scientific study of human and animal behavior). Genetics plays a large role in when and how learning, growing, and development occur. For example, although environment has an effect on the walking behavior of infants and toddlers, children are unable to walk at all before an age that is predetermined by their genome. However, while the genetic makeup of a child determines the age range for when he or she will begin walking, environmental influences determine how early or late within that range the event will actually occur."* [xiv]

The interaction of genetic endowment and the environment correlates with temperament and houses respectively in the model asserted by astrological psychology. The technique of dynamic calculations in astrological psychology determines whether the inherited traits find receptivity in the environment in a positive way or whether the environment stifles or inhibits genetic potential.

*Temperament* is the genetic construct that is based on research on heritable traits. There are dimensions of temperament in children based on monozygotic twin studies leading to identification of inherited traits. Scientists have found, for example, an *activity* level trait may be related to attention deficit disorder or the tendency to fear, anger and distress (negative emotionality and motor organization) can be related to *anxiety* and *neurotic* traits. Both behavior patterns can be correlated with the co-actions of specific combinations of genes. The response by the child's environment in reaction to these inherited behaviors can impact him negatively or positively depending on the reaction of his caretakers to his/her behavior.

> *"Although estimates of heritability tend to differ from sample to sample, they generally fall within the range of .20 to .60, suggesting that genetic differences among individuals account for approximately 20% to 60% of the variability of temperament within a population."*[xv]

For our purposes, we assume that temperament or genetics as revealed by the planets in signs in astrological psychology constitutes on average about 50% of the behavior potential of the child.

## Dynamic Calculations

Astrological psychology assumes that the placements of planets in signs reflect the genetic components contributing to the behavior of individuals. The numbers of planets in the houses determine the extent to which the environment plays a positive or negative role in the horoscope. The numbers of planets in signs compared to the numbers of planets in the houses determines whether one or the other has a dominant role in the behavior. According to astrological psychology, specific genetic traits (positive or negative) may be impacted by differences in the relative degrees of stressors in the environment and/or the lack of responsiveness and acceptance from the environment.

The metaphor of a mustard seed being planted among rocks is apt to make this point. Some seeds are planted in rocks and stunted in growth; others are planted in fertile soil with enough sun and rain to flourish. The exact birth time, date and place used to construct the horoscope reflect the specific hereditary and environmental factors for client analysis. Such stressors as societal demands and losses that don't support a person's genetic potentials, and neglect by the environment in recognizing inherited abilities, can contribute to problems for the client. These factors can lead to a client's maladaptive response of the environment.

Astrological psychology asserts that the *houses* in the horoscope represent the *environmental* influences. They are identified in a horoscope analysis through a preponderance of the distribution of planets in three motivations or qualities—cardinal, mutable or fixed—along with the preponderance of fire, air, earth or water elements. The planets in *signs* in the horoscope are directly correlated with *inherited temperament*; a preponderance of the distribution of planets in the three qualities and four temperaments: fire, earth, air and water will yield which temperament is predominant. Taken together, the total numbers of planets in signs constitute the temperament influence and the preponderance of planets in the houses constitute the environmental influence. The difference between the two sums, depending whether the house or sign total is larger, will determine whether the difference is positive or negative. If it is positive, the houses have more influence; if it is negative the signs have more influence.

> *"the planets in the signs and houses indicate how Man reacts to his environment: the configuration of aspects reflects states of consciousness, our inner motivations; the signs of the zodiac indicate genetic structure, the hereditary factors that a person brings into the world with him, to which the psychic, spiritual characteristics also belong."* [xvi]

The environment plays a major role in determining behavior but there are limits based on biology. Referring to the question of meeting the needs of children, specifically for love, safety, security and self-esteem, environmental factors interact with genetic traits to produce positive or negative outcomes impacting on behavior and adjustment. What, then, are the temperamental factors that weigh in to determine the ability of a child to adapt to environmental stressors?

In the dynamic calculations, normally performed by computer software, a total number is given either a plus or a minus to signify the degree of environmental pressure or lack of it on the constitution. A difference of above +25 signifies pressure to conform to the dictates of the outer world, whereas numbers from +5 to -25 signify that the energy brought by inheritance (sign) is greater than the environment wants, so that there is a surplus of untapped potential in the individual. The dynamic calculations can show how these attributes are over-formed or under-formed by the conditioning given to the child and the expectations put upon her by her environment. Traits are either over-formed or under-formed, and can have direct consequences on the gratification of needs for love, safety, and for self esteem.[xvii]

Below are the dynamic calculations for two individuals, Ale and Rick who have two different reactions of environment to their heredity potential.

**Rick**

| | Crosses-Motivation | | | | Elements-Temperament | | | |
|---|---|---|---|---|---|---|---|---|
| | Total | Cardinal | Fixed | Mutable | Fire | Earth | Air | Water |
| Signs | 104 | 17 | 60 | 27 | 42 | 22 | 32 | 8 |
| Houses | 152 | 82 | 39 | 31 | 20 | 36 | 55 | 41 |
| Diff. | +48 | 65 | -21 | 4 | -22 | 14 | 23 | 33 |

**Figure 2.2 Ricks dynamic calculations based on birth date, time, place**

In Rick's case, the sign (heredity) vs. house (environment) difference is +48 which means he can have a significant amount of stress caused by the environment and should watch his health when environmental stressors occur. These stressors can exhaust his constitution and cause illness. Rick has a Ph. D. in Administrative Education and is a retired Superintendent of Schools. By his own admission, he has had to protect himself from too many commitments with the environment to keep his health in balance. Rick's chart is below.

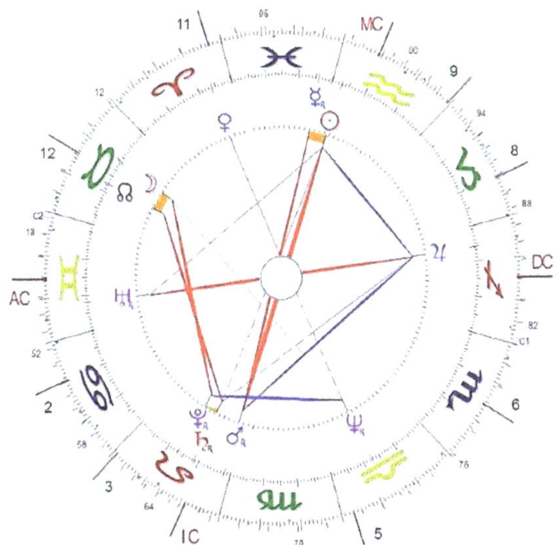


**Figure 3.2 Rick's Chart**

**Ale**

| | Crosses-Motivation | | | | Elements-Temperament | | | |
|---|---|---|---|---|---|---|---|---|
| | Total | Cardinal | Fixed | Mutable | Fire | Earth | Air | Water |
| Signs | 101 | 29 | 15 | 57 | 10 | 28 | 29 | 34 |
| Houses | 89 | 18 | 48 | 23 | 20 | 18 | 25 | 26 |
| Diff. | -12 | -11 | 43 | -34 | 10 | -10 | -4 | -8 |

**Figure 4.2 Ale's dynamic calculations based on birth date, time, place**

In Ale's case, the sign (heredity) vs. house (environment) difference is -12, indicating that the environment is not pressuring her but neither is it supportive of her genetic potential. A persistent theme in Ale's life has been that when she starts a project, the environment shows no interest. For example, Ale lives in Moscow and taught 'change agent management for corporations' at Moscow University, a subject relating to transitioning workers to new training and placement opportunities when corporations downsize. This study is not really relevant to an authoritarian environment such as Russia and her department was eventually abolished. The environment did not support her talents. This theme repeats itself in her life and could be discouraging. But the lesson of such predisposition is that Ale should not be seek approval from the outside world in relation to her talents; and she should not neglect these, but rather, try to develop these abilities for their own sake, not for the sake of pleasing others.

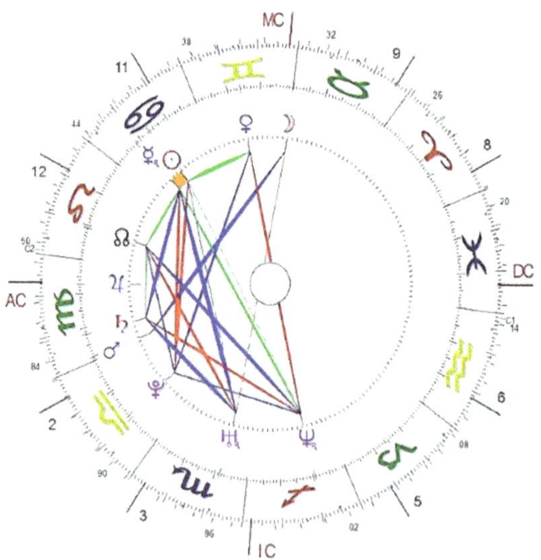


**Figure 5.2 Ale's Chart**

In summary, the development of the child into a mature functioning human being depends on how well he uses his genetic potential as he/she comes up against environmental pressures and opportunities. The parallels between Maslow's hierarchy of needs and planetary ego development provide insight into a treatment focus for clients when there are deficits. Identification of and support of the strongest ego planet's potential to work in the world, an awareness of which archetype energizes her capacities to reach her full potential, and dynamic calculation of the mix of environmental vs. genetic factors provides an understanding of the potential for healthy development.

## Toward a Psychology of being: self actualization

Transcendence of Maslow's and Erikson's models of 'normal development' and an individual's accomplishment of psychosocial tasks are necessary achievements leading to self-actualization. The model of astrological psychology asserts that it is not enough to develop a healthy ego. Achievement of a healthy ego is a precursor to the next stage of awareness: the deliberate realization of Self through understanding of the universal archetypes of the transcendental planets as they relate to and expand ego consciousness. Thus, the goal of self actualization involves putting some distance between one's ego needs and gratification of them, so that one can be receptive to higher levels of awareness.

Self-esteem that results from surmounting the crises and opportunities, brought about by achievement of psychosocial tasks, is the foundation for the next step in awareness—self-actualization. It is true that a degree of intuition is needed to be motivated toward achieving non-material goals. A yearning based on the realization that there is something more, beyond mere ego gratification, can be realized once basic needs are met. Identification with spiritual and universal principles is beyond the scope of our self-interest in individual ego gratifications alone (see Figure 1.2, page 42).

A consultation using astrological psychology's AP progression and transits can trigger the potential for reaching an awareness that there are higher states yet to be developed beyond the levels of ego attachments. States of consciousness that are beyond healthy ego development and good self-esteem can set the stage for one to enter the transpersonal realm of spiritual awareness. The consultant is tasked to re-frame the threats to ego integrity that identification with transcendental realms represent and, at the same time, reinforce for the client what she has already accomplished. Steps to prepare a client for awareness of the ascent into higher realms of consciousness require preparation and discipline. There are stages of awakening on the way to psychosynthesis and awareness to the transpersonal self between the field of consciousness and the middle and higher levels of the unconscious (see Assagioli's Egg, Figure 3, page 10).

Roberto Assagioli stated that spiritual awareness is dependent on a number of qualities that require discipline such as the following:

> *"...the capacity for introversion (deeply reflecting and documenting inner life unfolding); going deeper into our own shadow nature and not being overwhelmed by fear; ascent to higher levels through sublimation of passions and instincts; understanding the nature of mental and emotional illusions leading to continual errors of judgment, wrong behaviors and suffering of all kinds; to become disentangled (through a process of dis-identification with the our mental thoughts, our body sensations and our emotional reactions); seeing ourselves as spiritual beings and developing spiritual potentials through para-psychological abilities; developing universal love beyond patriotism and love of our place of birth; pilgrimage to holy places; understanding the symbolism of our dreams resulting in transmutation; liberation and freedom from fear, having abilities to see connections to all beings through initiation."* [xviii]

Introversion is a process of withdrawing energy from the outside world and deliberately investing in thoughts, images and feelings that go on inside one's Self. It is an introspective process which includes journal-writing and dream diary recording, reflecting on our life's narrative and finding meaning in our own ethical point of view.[xix]

As a result of working with sub-personalities, dreams and fantasies on the journey to the personal unconscious, we confront our shadows as the dark sides of our personality. Our shadow elements on this dark side are usually suppressed and repressed, and hidden from our awareness. We do not show these shadow entities to other people because they contain shameful, disgusting desires and passions. Each shadow can represent a split off entity and energy that the ego judges as not worthy of bringing into the light; so we often project these unwanted traits onto others. A shadow can also be a sub-personality. But we can learn to 'own' our shadows and can do this through withdrawing projections of what we find as unacceptable behavior in others and owning the possibility that those qualities we despise are actually part of us and our desire nature.[xx]

Sublimation is a defense mechanism into which the individual drives such instincts and impulses as, for example, anger, lust, and power, transmuting them into creative actions such as athletics and art forms, thus adding to our ability to enrich the non-material sides of our natures.[xxi]

The realization that, even though we experience reality through our senses, mental thoughts and feelings, ultimately, these are illusions that cause suffering when we identify with them too much, is the Hindu concept referred to as *Maya.* Ego attachment to these illusions creates a cycle of repetition that is ultimately unrewarding and impedes our way to a higher state of awareness on our spiritual quest.[xxii]

Through meditation we can learn to dis-identify from our sensations, mental images, thoughts and feelings. By practicing sitting still for 30 minutes daily, for example, we can reduce ego attachments by transcending thoughts which prompt us to act, we can learn to ignore bodily discomforts that make us change position and emotional reactions that disturb our equanimity. Such lessons in self-observation can translate into a less stressed and reactive life-style.[xxiii]

Through understanding our dreams, we can find connections to pre-cognitions, clairvoyance over distances, and psychic impressions that enrich our knowledge of the world and deepen our conviction that we live in a spiritual and non-material world where synchronicity is the law that governs behavior, and not only cause and effect.[xxiv] I expand on this concept in chapter three.

Belief in the equality of all people, their accomplishments and suffering, from all ethnic groups and races of peoples all over this planet is another preparation for transcendence. The division of human species into 'races' is partly conventional and partly arbitrary and does not imply any hierarchy whatsoever. This is confirmed by travel and learning the culture and language of other peoples, not by believing in the concept of race as a barrier to identification with others and seeing the cultural relativity of one own ethnic world-view.[xxv]

Amplification and study of dreams beyond their personal records to associations and expansions of meaning as universal archetypes can have significance from a cultural-historical perspective that reaches beyond time, space and dimension into the realm of divine guidance.[xxvi] Chapter 3 explains this connection.

The realization that fear is a defense against material loss of safety and security enables us to embrace the belief that as spiritual beings God loves us so much that she/he would protect us even unto and after death itself; and that we live on eternally and will be re-incarnated into another form so that we can continue to grow spiritually.[xxvii]

## Initiation rituals

In these modern times, we have lost touch with the rituals of antiquity which served the purpose of bringing people into social membership and guiding the initiate's development through practices that have a tradition and deep wisdom. No longer are there opportunities for a committee of elders to benevolently guide us through a process in which we achieve individual leaps of consciousness. Unfortunately, we sometimes experience this transpersonal realm through ingestion of hallucinogenic drugs but without the cultural context and support to interpret the experience in a personally transformative manner leading to a transmutation of consciousness.

We have to achieve this ourselves, often on a lonely journey though practices that change consciousness such as trance-like states from meditation, magical associations, visitations and 'possessions' by angels and demons as manifested in dreams. In 400 BCE, there were dream temples and Asclepius, the god of medical arts, was worshipped all over the Greek civilization. His temples and ministers were believed to have healing powers. He was thought to reveal how to cure diseases through dreams. Thus people would go to these temples and have dreams interpreted when they were sick. The divine inspiration of the God Asclepius had a healing effect. These practices helped enthusiastically to promote the power of dreams and detachment of the individual from material reality to facilitate entry into the phenomenological world.

The goals of initiation are: developing the ability to see through our fearful attachments, letting go of conflicts; purification of selfishness, denying the duality of love and hate; learning forgiveness; increasing faith, self-realization, creative thinking, and application of the will.

Abraham Maslow's hierarchy of needs identifies that certain basic needs must be met before one can ascend to the realm of self-actualized consciousness. Huber in *The Planets* recognizes that initiation at this level of consciousness can begin with certain initiatory rituals concerning the transcendent planets Uranus, Neptune and Pluto in transit aspect to the ego planets, Saturn, Moon, and Sun. Obviously, the basic needs for food, shelter, etc. must have been met first.

Now we will focus on those initiatory rituals defined by Huber, how to identify them in transits as triggers, and what kind of expansion of consciousness we can expect from such initiations. When the AP aspects by transit the transcendental planets—Uranus, Neptune or Pluto—and when a transit of one of these planets aspects a natal ego planet then, as Bruno and Louise Huber identified, three pathways of initiation are possible. If the natal horoscope has transcendent planets in aspect to ego planets, one should consider the initiate's receptivity to these paths as open to a possibility for transcendence. We will examine three horoscopes which by aspects of these transcendent planets to ego planets provide a pathway to initiation through a dis-identification with the three ego states as follows.

**Saturn and Uranus pathway to initiation.**

To develop faith and reduce doubt is the goal of the first initiation. When we are disturbed by our material dependency, our physical conditionality, and decide we want to be happy rather than dwell on worrying about possible losses, then the needs for security and safety are subordinated to the insight that there are creative paths where convictions about the value of innovation, possible utopia and intelligence guide the way.

A metaphor is Christ's birth coincident with the killing of the innocents, and the persecution that awaited Him. Christ had new insights: he brought love, redemption and forgiveness into the world. There could be no doubt that Christ led the way to a new world view.

Another metaphor of the way of individuation is Saul's conversion to Paul on the road to Damascus when he became a disciple. He made a new commitment to follow Jesus and gave up his old life as a tax collector, even though he was secure in his old role. Paul then abandoned security to follow Christ, and he abandoned the tradition of Judaism.

During this transformation, an individual is aware that he is responsible for all men. He puts his physical body in a state to be of service to his God. The practice of Yoga fits into this conversion of the body so that it becomes a vehicle for the soul or Atman to shine through. When the AP transits or passes Saturn and Uranus, we can expect this kind of transformation. The people who have Saturn and Uranus conjunct in their natal horoscopes also are sensitive to this type of transformation.[xxviii]

## Hannah

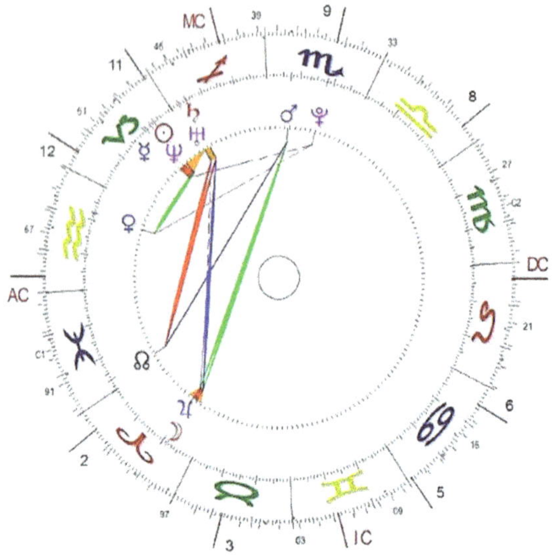


**Figure 6.2 Hannah's chart**

Hannah has Uranus and Saturn conjunct behind the 11th house cusp in her natal horoscope. Saturn is at the low point in the 10th, which gives her an insecure voice in asserting her needs for security and safety to others. Uranus is stressed just before the 11th house. Other configurations in her natal chart reinforce Hannah's lack of self-assertion and silence regarding her ideals, thoughts and values (North Node in 1st house intercepted). She may have doubts about opportunities in the environment to support her thinking, and take refuge in routines that let others lead the way while she quietly acquiesces. She might benefit from an initiation that gives her more confidence in her own thinking and converts her style from passivity into speaking out about her ideals and philosophy; but the motivation for doing so may be lacking unless she makes a 100% commitment to asserting herself with energy, no matter what others might think. She could benefit from rituals in which she could find her own voice and assert herself in a safe environment as a rehearsal for real life. Then she could purposefully put herself in public speaking situations where she can assert her ideals by testing them in the outside world. It would mean a complete change in her style of relating, which up to this time has been quietly blossoming but not publically expressed.

**Neptune and the Moon pathway to initiation.**

The path of Neptune and the Moon speaks to the experience of love and suffering that one must go through in relationships when one subordinates one's ego for another. This initiation leads to the subsequent refinement of the ego needs. When one does not get reciprocal sympathy and unconditional love, yet still loves and forgives another, this changes consciousness. Ego based love is conditional and selfish. But when one suffers from a betrayal of love and yet still continues to love without resentment and is able to forgive, then one is able to elevate ones emotions beyond petty ego wants and desires. He/she can transcend opposites and avoid the projection that promotes conflict; because emotional identification with either extreme of two opposites can bring resentment. This requires a dis-identification from the emotional ego.

The suffering of the ego and its' 'death' brings about the dark night of the soul, causing one to feel abandoned and hopeless. As a purification experience, Christ was baptized to love all people, despite being persecuted. Through the betrayal of Judas and his crucifixion, He was able to forgive those who persecuted him.

Because the experience of suffering and continuing to love is a continual process throughout the life cycle, there is an ongoing struggle to let go of the childish ego for the sake of ideal love. The passing phase of being betrayed and forsaken can last a long time and, during this process of purification, we are asked to let go of hope and what we consider are legitimate demands of reciprocal love. This process puts one in a completely different situation and changes consciousness. One surrenders to God's will and that process is transformative. Transits of Neptune to an ego planet can trigger these experiences and crises.[xxix]

## Eileen

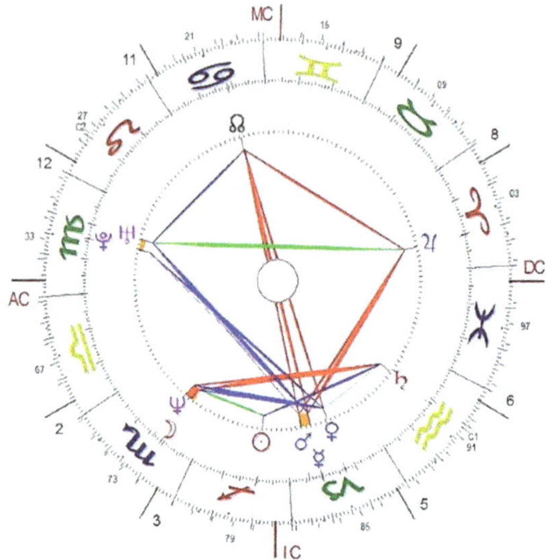


**Figure 7.2 Eileen's chart**

Eileen has been divorced for 2 years and, recently, her mother passed away. She had a difficult marriage in which she had to serve her husband's immature needs for years while raising her children almost on her own. She would rescue her husband many times in their relationship and prop him up (Neptune conjunct Moon Natal chart). Last year she was betrayed by him. He refused to grow up and take responsibilities in the family, and he left her. Her mother, to whom she was close, passed away around that same time.

Now her children have grown up and left home, and her former husband has divorced her and is remarried to a foreign national. Eileen, feeling abandoned and forsaken, is experiencing the dark night of the soul. Yet she is open to finding new energy to trust in her ex, and to love again. For example, during recent holidays, she invited her ex along with his new wife to a family dinner. They attended and, although awkward for Eileen, she responded to her higher nature. This represents the change in consciousness from bitterness through purification to the ability to forgive and try to love again.

**Pluto and the Sun pathway to initiation.**

The initiation path of correct thinking, in spite of temptations to give up and abandon the will, is the way of transfiguration and higher consciousness. This implies that one aligns the power of the personality to the one goal of controlling one's thoughts, so as to create one's own image of the world. This way is much like the Christ's *Via Dolorosa*, the way of the cross. Christ went through fourteen stations and many ego states on His way to the cross: joyless, discouraged that his life was meaningless, in physical and emotional pain, unable to rest or quench His thirst, He was exhausted by the time He reached the cross. At the apex of this suffering, one finds the light of harmony of his being one with God. In order for this transformation to occur, there has to be a decrease in identification with the Sun ego and a humility. In fact, one must reach down to the core of one's being, to the depths of one's soul, and relinquish the personal will so as to align it to the Divine will. *'Father, unto You I commend my spirit!'* Transits of Pluto, Neptune or Uranus to the natal ego planets, in combination with the intelligent planets of Jupiter and Mercury, can test one's resolve to set down the egocentric stance and be reduced to only what the Divine will ordains.[xxx]

## John

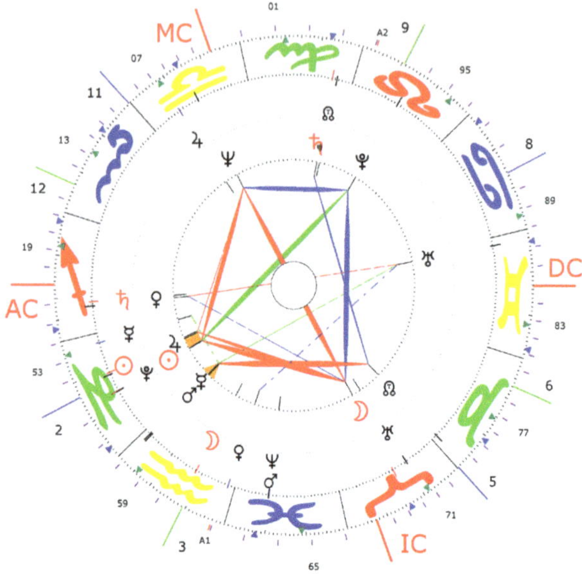


**Figure 8.2 John's chart showing Pluto transiting natal Sun**

*Outer ring shows transiting planets, inner ring radix planets.*

John (Figure 8.2) has been ambivalent about the power of his own thinking, struggling to overcome self-delusions and fears about his emotion-based projections (natal Moon opposition Neptune). He has been delaying his commitment to enter the spiritual path. Now he is trying to think for himself and willing his temptations to cease about abandoning his daily disciplines. He is practicing meditation and creating a positive image of the world he wants for himself. This mental steadfastness is difficult because the planet Pluto is transiting in conjunction with his natal Sun (1/2017), and he has become aware of the diversions that prompt him to stray from the straight and narrow path of daily yoga and meditation. He has to confront distortions daily and use his will consistently to create the positive thoughts and actions he wants, in spite of environmental set-backs and insecurities. But to go forward means abandoning fear and controlling his thoughts of negativity.

**Conclusion:**

The accomplishment of life tasks opens developmental opportunities that may eventually help the individual along the path to a transpersonal level of consciousness. Assisted by the drives for transcendence of the ego represented by Uranus, Neptune and Pluto, one can intuit and accept an eventual detachment from the very ego bonds that supported individuality leading to maturity.

Certain ego challenges from the environment certainly do inhibit ego integration, especially when social pressures are greater than one's inherited potential, or there is an adverse environment that inhibits the good traits that might be expressed. In addition, the frustration of the ego's drives for realization through betrayal, doubt and mental distractions can hamper the application of a person's will to build a spiritual life.

Since we have lost those rites of passage in Western cultures that reflect initiation into society, counselors and astrologers could be well advised to draw attention to them, when they are relevant to their clients. In the later stages of life, cultural practices and social evolution may include promoting qualities of character and practices that prepare our clients for inner growth. Because initiation rituals can change the focus of consciousness and reverse low self esteem and feelings of victimization, we can choose to build on the acceptance of these tests and support our clients' need for self-actualization.

# Chapter 3. Capturing Dreaming Events

*Stars shining bright above you,*
*Night breezes seem to whisper, 'I love you,'*
*Birds singing in the sycamore tree*
*Dream a little dream of me.*
*Say, 'night-ie night' and kiss me*
*Just hold me tight and tell me you'll miss me,*
*While I'm alone and blue as can be,*
*Dream a little dream of me…*

Mamas and Pappas, Fabian Andre,
Gus Kuhn, Wilbur Schwandt

This chapter will identify the nature of dreaming patterns in a night's sleep, the pre- and post-sleep influences on daily events before and after a dream, and how to enhance dream recall. Specific features of dreaming that make it worthwhile to work with the remembered dream[i] will be highlighted. The real work required of the dreamer to reveal the meaning of the dream will be explained. The limitations of solitary dream work and ways to improve dream recall and amplification of dream symbolism are covered.[ii]

## The Dreaming Brain

Jung believed that interpretation of dreams was of little use in isolation but better in a series;[iii] the fact is that we dream every night with a succession of images, and some stand out more than others. My work with dreams recommends that we record a series of dreams in a night. For practical purposes, we work with one set of images that captures what we want to explore. The later dreams correct the mistakes made in handling those that went before in a given night. So, although it appears in this work that one dream appears to be worked on alone, it is actually chosen as the best example in a night's dream series.

We dream every night but not the whole night through. The physiology of sleep, as measured by Electroencephalograms (EEG's), demonstrates that there are two major phases of brain-wave patterns measured and they are: rapid eye movement (REM) or the absence of REM or NONREM. REM brain-wave patterns have short amplitudes (height of the wave), are sharper, and have closer frequency patterns like a saw's teeth. The deep sleep stages of NONREM sleep have Delta and K-complex brain-wave patterns that show wider frequency patterns and long amplitudes.[iv]

REM sleep is reported to be connected to dreaming with the most vivid imagery and emotional involvement, whereas NONREM sleep reflects more subdued thought patterns.[v] The total amount of time spent dreaming is about 90 minutes during a night's eight-hour sleep. The dreaming frequency for an eight-hour sleep is split up into about four segments of REM dreaming. The final time of REM dreaming sleep occurs just before awakening and lasts from 25 to 45 minutes. There are departures from this pattern. However, research shows that our most productive dream creation REM sleep is during the time immediately before we awaken, and that we are most likely to remember those dreams after awakening.[vi]

## The settings influence on dreams

Dream research reveals controversial findings between laboratory-studied dream research and home-studied dream research. Proponents of controlled laboratory studies such as Foulkes and Wisez[vii] assert that the laboratory studies provide the most representative examples for the study of the important questions relating to the nature of dream content. They take a strictly cognitive behavioral approach, saying that the sleeping mind is not functionally different from the waking mind. Furthermore, they do not believe in an unconscious mind at all. But research also shows that dreams studied in the home environment are significantly preferable to study, because they occur in a natural environment. Furthermore, home dreams contain more elements of the dreamer as befriender, more sexual interactions and more emotional content than lab reports.[viii] Obviously, a more naturalistic setting can produce a more relaxed and emotionally compatible setting for dreaming.

Globus indicates an opposition to the mechanistic view of the cognitive behavioral lab dream research and takes an existential phenomenological approach to the meaning of dreams that is consistent with my view.

> *"The dreaming life-world is created de novo. Thus our dreams are first hand creations, rather than put together from residues of waking life. We have the capacity for infinite creativity; at least while dreaming, we partake of the power of the immanent Spirit, the infinite Godhead that creates the cosmos. In waking, we "contract away from infinity", as Wilber says, and take a Heideggerian "fall" into a limited life world."* [ix]

This view is consistent with the premise of astrological psychology that supports the work of physicist David Bohm, from the University of London and a former colleague of Einstein, who expanded on the hologram model of the universe to suggest that the information of the entire universe is contained in each of its parts. Bohm believed in an implicate order of the physical universe which is an invisible enfolded reality and underlies the external manifestations.[x] So that what is above is reflected in what is below; what is outside is reflected by what is inside. All the world's possibilities are enfolded in the 'object,' according to Globus[xi] the dream represents a microcosmic reflection of the universal one-mind, and to ignore the guidance from the source of all things would be a mistake.

## Pre and Post Sleep Influence on dreams

Watching action movies right before going to bed, having stressful interactions with others and, for example, having pre-operative or pre-public speaking anxiety intensifies the use of adaptive mechanisms in people so that they have dreams that balance psychological dis-equilibrium.[xii] Because a dream's content is affected by immediate daily stressors, it is recommended that we are prepared to recognize the impact of these variables in dream content, especially because the most recent impressions are most commonly manifested in dreams at the beginning of the night.[xiii]

I recommend a quiet lifestyle in preparation for a night's sleeping. Following sleep hygiene techniques[xiv] to calm the body and mind right before sleeping can soothe the concerns of the day: journaling, taking a hot soaking bath, keeping bright lights at a minimum and avoiding over-stimulating movies right before bed may help to work through adaptive strategies and emotional concerns that occur during waking life.

## How to enhance dream recall before and after sleep

### Exercise 1

Will Parfitt applied dream work in psychosynthesis and considered it a spiritual practice. Entering the dream world and convincing yourself that dreams are worthy of exploration can be enhanced by alternating your awareness between dreams and reality.

Parfitt asks you to remember an important dream from any time in your life, and to ask yourself what was the most exciting and fulfilling dream you had: write this dream down and visualize a scene as if this dream were happening now. Building in as much detail of the dream as possible is recommended.

Then he tells us to think about the dream and alternate thinking about it with looking at our hands. Alternate your attention between the dream imagery and the visual experience of looking at your hands. Keep returning to look at your hands each time the dream image fades and continue this exercise for as long as this feels comfortable.

Consider what this image has to tell you or teach you now. Repeat this process each night before going to bed and say to yourself, 'I am awake within this dream.'[xv]

The purpose of this exercise is to blend waking life and dream life together since we could be dreaming while we are awake.

**Exercise 2**

Preparations before bedtime can include meditations on the affirmations of psychosynthesis to decrease self-identification. We do this because we want to be receptive to the cosmos, not guided by ego-centric interests, desires or passions. Will Parfitt, in his chapter on Spiritual Growth and Meditation,[xvi] has instructed us to use a meditation to dis-identify with body, emotions and mind. After we participate in relaxation exercises such as progressive muscle relaxation and deep breathing (See Appendix on page 77), we can repeat the following affirmations before retiring:

I have a body and sensations and I am more than my body.

I have feelings and I am more than my feelings and emotions.

I have a mind and thoughts and I am more than my mind and thoughts.[xvii]

You may have to repeat this exercise nightly using this script but you can memorize it once you practice. The effort is worth it because the external influences that distracted you, your wants and desires will have less a hold on you as your prepare for dreaming.

You should prepare a dream diary for use the next day. The contents of this should include sections called:

a. Dream diary in which you record series of dreams as D1, D2, D3, etc. in one night.

b. Previous Days and current Day's events

c. Dream amplification section

d. Drawings

Dream work requires discipline and preparation but it is well worth the effort for the insights it brings, as it bridges your conscious and unconscious minds.

Do not use an alarm clock to wake up. Do not move physically upon awakening but enter into a reverie and try to recollect the night's dreams. Be open to the images of your dreaming time. Keep your dream diary beside your bed so you can write it down immediately upon awakening and recalling it. Report the dream in your dream diary exactly as it occurred without interpretation.[xx] Later, at the end of the day, work on amplification of the dreams, following steps 7-10 on page 68.

**Here are some steps to follow to recover your dream, report it and amplify it:**

1. On awakening, write in your daily log: How did you feel upon awakening? Do this whether in the middle of the night or in the morning.
2. Write down the dream images as they occur and date them.
3. Give the dream a name, but save it for later after the full detail in your dream amplification section is completed.
4. Each dream has a beginning, an action section, and an ending.
5. During the day, or at end of day record the day's events, and in response to the movement of your emotions.
6. Record your thoughts and feelings related to the previous day.
7. Reread the dream of today.
8. Close your eyes, breathe deeply, and go to the dream amplification section. Wait. In your mind's eye re-enter the dream of the day and continue to be aware of images, feelings and actions in the dream. Now on the screen of your mind's eye, guide the development of the dream. You do not restrict or direct this process. Record associations with people, places and things in our life–in the dream amplification section.
9. Stop and reread what you have written so far. Become aware of the feelings and emotions in You, as those experiences were taking place.
10. If you wish, I recommend you draw a dream image that grabs you. Date and title the drawing.

Consider some key questions for the amplification section: What was the atmosphere and tone that accompanied the dream? What awareness is kindled in you? Is the dream communicating a message to you? Do you perceive hints and indicators as you read it back? Have a dialogue with a character in your dream; between your dream ego and a character (see, Ira Progoff, *At a Journal Workshop*).[xviii] With a recurrent, distressing or traumatic dream, relax and imagine a different ending to the dream and write it down.[xix]

## Specific features of the remembered dream that make it worthwhile to work with the dream

Montague Ullman noted three features of dreams that motivate one to enter the work of self-analysis of dreams:

> *"The first important feature of dreaming is its relevance to our current life… feeling residues of recent experiences surface when our brain gets the signal to start dreaming… The second important feature is our ability to gather more information relevant to a current issue than we can readily do when awake… The third important feature of the dreaming psyche is the profoundly honest way in which a dream reflects our subjective state."* [xxi]

Dreamwork requires using the language of visual metaphor to discern a dream's secret. It is not always straightforward and requires detailed work on the text. Not only are the associational contexts of dreams difficult to relate to, but there is a play on words that often comes into our awareness.

Age Point aspects and the day's events and associations feed into a person's personal unconscious to affect dream content. Dreams actively and passively stimulate complexes in the personal unconscious through the archetype of the Self (Figures 1.3 below, 2.3 page 71). A complex is an emotionally charged group of ideas or images. At the center of a complex is an archetype or archetypal image (which contains contents of opposites, like masculine and feminine, strong or weak, ect.).[xxii]

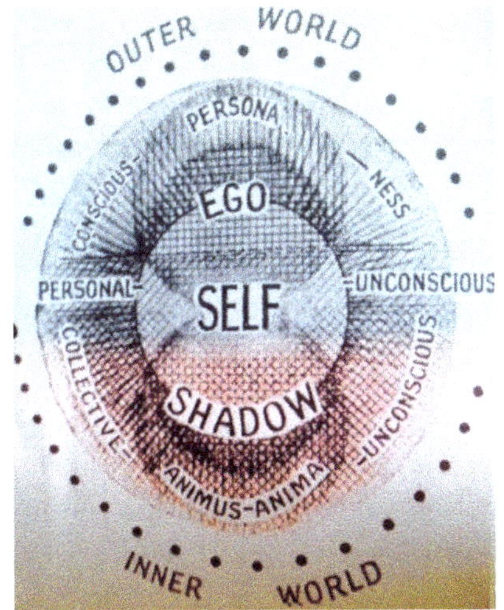


**Figure 1.3. Jacobi, Jolande, C.G. Jung,**
Yale University Press, New Haven, London1973, p. 130

A dream may improve or worsen an identity pattern such as, for example, making the dreamer feel dominant or submissive. Dream images do this by changing a number of inter-related complexes arranged in a net-like structure in the personal unconscious that affects the ego identity of the dreamer. The ego identity is not fixed and can be changed by a dream image acting on it. The ego identity of the dreamer is so involved that it gets changed by the Self in this process.

The ego plays an important role in generating dreams also, as it illuminates complexes through a process of creating or dissolving them based on the events of the day. And the Self, as the organizing principle or the archetype of order in the psyche plays a role in changing the ego identity as well.[xxiii]

Thus we have a complete feedback loop from the day's events, AP and transit aspects to the horoscope, affecting the dream images, which stimulate complexes, which in turn change the ego identity of the dreamer, based on his/her strongest ego planet's capacity for dealing with these changes.

Not only can daily events change the content of dreams by interacting with complexes, but dreams can also come from forces inside the personal unconscious.

> *"The structure of complexes can be altered by The Self… both directly (as in a particular dream content coming from an unconscious complex) or indirectly through the Self leading the ego to face certain conflicts or growth stages that the individual has tried to avoid. Both the ego (in its interaction with the outside world) and the Self, therefore, can influence the structure of complexes (through dreams) upon which the ego relies for one's sense of identity."* [xxiv]

Theoretically, the Self is located within the central core of the horoscope.[xxv] The Self highlights a current ego identity usually guided by dreams and triggered by AP progressions and transits to a sensitive point in the chart. The dynamic interplay of the archetype of the Self with the ego complex 'charges' the current identity of the individual. In this way ego contents are changed. These changes come from the force of the Self or central core. Thus the Self can illuminate a complex that is usually unconscious thereby leading a person to change his ego identity (Figure 2.3).

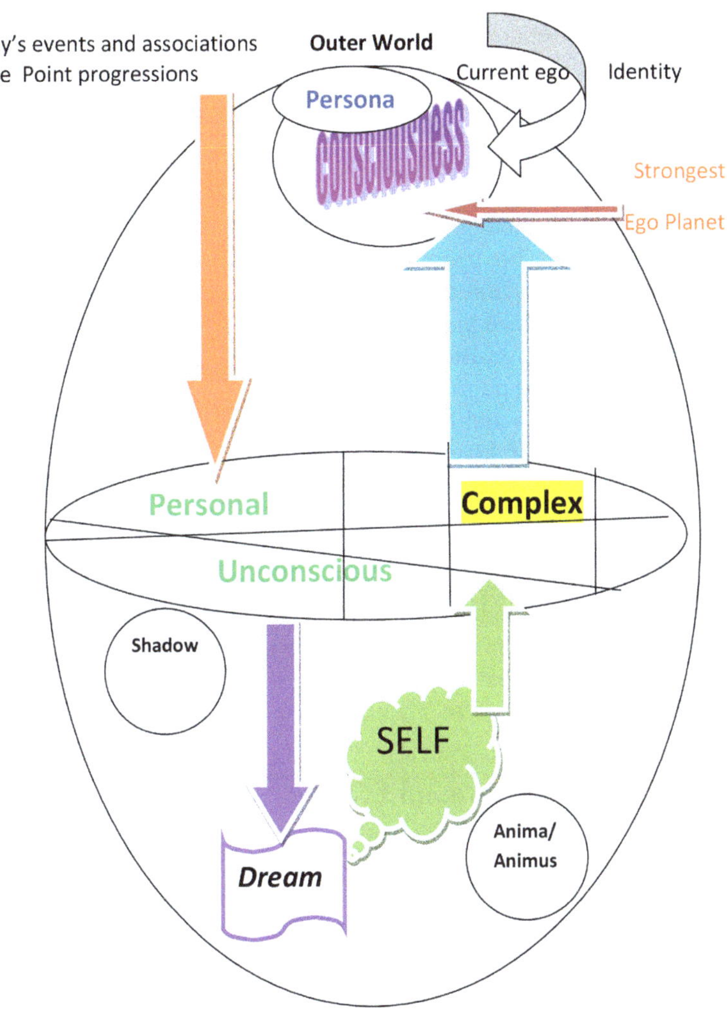


**Figure 2.3 Inner World**

For example, if the AP transit is in the 10th house and opposite the natal Sun in the 4th house, this aspect may stimulate an increased independence and activity directed toward goals. One may dream of being on a mountain top viewing one's domain. The dream stimulates the Self which, in turn, innervates the complex, which may contain the dominance/submission archetype. The dominance archetype imbues the ego planet of the Sun with energy, which influences the identity of the person to be more publically forthright and commanding. This may be in contrast to the usual ego identity of the person with the natal Sun in the 4th house. If the AP is in the 10th house, the Huber life phase is 'Authority and Individuation—Call to Self-Realization',[xxvi] and the developmental challenge could be to call on traits that enhance independence, thinking and achievement.

The above is consistent with our focus on relating dreams to psychological crisis points as the AP progresses. We have chosen only those conjunctions and oppositions of APs aspecting sensitive chart areas. Psychological drives symbolized by the planets represent energy in the psyche, and these aspects reflect what is happening to the ego identity of the person as the Self directs the process of adaptation to the environment necessary to deal with a life challenge.

After the decks are cleared and the scene calms down, the ego identity of the individual dreamer can be changed, as a result of the new insights brought about by this process. This is one reason why dreamwork is so valuable when working with AP progression, because both work in concert to change the lives of the individual—one reinforces the other.

## Real work on dream amplification:

We are involved in expanding the definition of certain scenes in a dream by making associations to their content. When we have a scene with elements of a dream, a story, or theme, there emerges an ending. We would break down that scene to make associations with various elements of the dream by relating them to images, symbols, autobiographical events, or contexts in our lives previous to the dream.

**On 1/19/2014 I had a dream**

> *'I was going to climb a mountain with some people. We were ascending but I needed clothes. I needed pants and long underwear. I had a paper bag of money (cash) in which I was going to buy provisions in a store. I left the other people I was with to find my gear and got a sense of relief from this. As I wandered through the store alone, I picked up my underwear and jeans. After a discussion with a clerk about something unimportant, I got in line to pay for my stuff. At once, I realized that I lost my paper bag of money. It was gone. I went looking for it. I went back behind the counters and thought one of the clerks took it. I could not find it anywhere. In the end, I discovered that I had the jeans and the underwear on a table and they belonged to me all along. I did not have to pay for them.'*

This dream contains elements which have to do with a new adventure—retirement, which occurred on 1/31/2014. The context of the dream was that I was retiring from working for 29 years in a job in which I played a dominant administrative role. I was going to have about half my income upon retirement, so in this story there is anxiety about being able to pay my way in preparation for this adventure.

My ego identity was also going to be changed drastically by retirement. I had to be prepared to work on inner armor (underwear) to deal with that change. Just like everybody else, I had to deal with payment for my goods, but I felt I would not have the resources to pay for my stuff.

In the end, I did not have to worry because the goods belonged to me all along. So in retirement, I was re-assured by this dream that there would be enough resources to deal with my new status as a retired elder. Further amplification revealed that the life phase I was going through at age 65 is called the 'Retirement age, the Beginning of the Aging Processes.' [xxvii] This is the time when *'most working people leave their careers and begin retirement. It also brings a decrease in social life. There is a big increase in deaths (retirement shock) at age 65.'* [xxviii] How synchronistic that the dream, the AP progression, and my actual retirement which occurred during the same month!

## Drawing your dream

Another method of amplification that is really helpful is to draw your dreams. The images can convey directly what visual metaphors were created in dreamtime and offer insights from the nonverbal realm.

### 9/06/2009

From a dream in which *'I look at a photograph album of my family. I remark after seeing this image of a boy on a bed that someone has been held in this room which is locked and secret as if in a cage. The boy was deprived of life and abused.'*

**Figure 3.3**

In this dream I was given an image spontaneously. I don't know who in my family it represents, but it may have been my father. He was the next to the youngest in his family and physically the smallest of five boys. My inference is that this dream referred to my dad, and was based on family pictures in which, as a boy, he is pictured with a frown. He always had issues with being of small stature and compensated for it by building strength and testing himself physically. Eventually he became addicted to alcohol and closed off communication to others about his issues from his past.

The dream image depicts the isolation and incarceration of the boy that could have triggered depression in my dad. Dad never discussed this possibility with me, nor had it ever become open discussion in my family. My father was accused (after his death) of, on multiple occasions, sexually abusing his 8-year-old granddaughter.

Because of my niece's symptoms of PTSD and substance-use disorder, I did not dismiss these accusations. I reasoned that the detailed descriptions of the sexual abuse by my niece could lead to a possibility that dad was abused himself. As is often the case, his possible history of previous abuse could be re-enacted by him abusing her. It is often the case with PTSD issues that the abused in turn becomes an abuser.

This dream picture represents an integration of the invisible with the visible, but without any information about the waking environment.[xxix] It came out of the blue, and the daily context was very difficult to describe because there was none. My father had died in 1979 and I was 60 at the time of the dream.

Further investigation shows, by using the AP progression, that maybe the dream referred to me. At that time that the AP was conjunct with my South Node at 2 degrees Scorpio in the 11th house, on the Relationship Axis. From this information, another possible interpretation of this dream emerges. Because the South Node represents the cumulative past lives of an individual and his 'Achilles heel', this dream could refer to my past lives of continuous transformation strewed with violent endings based on physical or sexual abuse. This could represent a fragment from cumulative past lives of mine in which I had allowed physical or sexual abuse of myself or others to continue brewing within my soul. The South Node can be quicksand: safe enough to look back into as long as no physical steps are taken in that direction.[xxx] This could indicate scenes from my past lives, which I had repressed.

**Limitations of solitary dream work:**

My wife and I have been sharing our dreams with each other for 40 years. It is valuable to get another perspective, and I have gotten help from her to make relevant current and past contexts that pertain to my dreams. My dream interpretations were clarified many times through our discussions. There are dream groups, which people can join, and these might be very satisfying, as long as certain group norms are observed as in the following:

> *"The safety of the* dreamer *who shares a dream would be in control of the process. In its effort to provide assistance, the group (or dyad) should always follow the associative track offered by the dreamer and never lead him/her… to maintain the dreamer's control, certain constraints on the group should include—no leading questions, the group must respect the privacy of the dreamer… They should never superimpose an interpretation on the dreamer… All interpretative ideas, be they right or wrong, should be considered as projections on the part of the person offering them unless they are accepted as meaningful by the dreamer… all participants including the leader should share their dreams so that the group structure is flattened and lessens dependency on the leader, and diminishes her role as authority."* [xxxi]

Solitary dream work is not a satisfactory outcome of interior dream research because as the I Ching says:

> *"Knowledge should be a refreshing and vitalizing force. It becomes so only through stimulating intercourse with congenial friends with whom one holds both discussion and practices application of the truths of life. In this way learning becomes many-sided and takes on a cheerful lightness, whereas there is always something ponderous and one-sided about the learning of the self-taught."* [xxxii]

## Appendix Muscle Relaxation and Breath Control

### A. Deep Progressive Muscle Relaxation

1. Lay on your back with palms up and legs extended. Remove all confining waist clothes like pants snaps, buckles, belts so that the stomach area is free to rise and contract.

2. Starting with the right foot, raise the right leg above the floor 8 inches. Point the toes toward your forehead so that your calf muscles become tight. Hold for 10 seconds. Let down the leg and foot and really relax it when it rests on the floor, make it limp.

3. Repeat with the left foot. It is important to let the foot totally relax when this "hold phase" is over

4. Next push your buttocks into the floor or bed until your stomach muscles become hard. Hold for 10 seconds and release. Take a deep breath and let it out. Relax and pay attention to the whole bottom of your body as it is limp and totally relaxed.

5. Next straighten out your arms as your sides and push them into your sides as hard as possible. Hold them for 8 seconds in this position. Now relax them and make them fall to your side palm up. Take a deep breath and let it out.

6. Next stick your tongue out and make a grimace, making your eyes squint and hold this position for 10 seconds. Relax your face muscles.

7. Now scan your whole body. Directing your attention to your feet, legs and calves. Your stomach arms and face have the muscles in a state of deep muscle relaxation.

## B. Pranayama (Breath Control)

1. Loosen your belt or clothes around your waist.

2. Put your thumb on your belly button with fingers extending down for your pubic area.

3. Now inhale to your lungs using your diaphragm muscle until your stomach and lungs are totally distended and count the number of seconds this takes till your full of breath.

4. Hold your breath for as long as you can comfortably do so. Count the seconds that you hold your breath

5. Now exhale your breath out through your nostrils and count the seconds it takes for you to let all the air out.

6. Note: repeat as many times as you want

Benefits: This is wonderful for hyperventilation a symptom of panic attacks, anger or anxiety. It slows down breathing allows for a good oxygen exchange with the blood in the body and brain and helps you by focusing on counting your breath rather than on your problems.

# Chapter 4. Using Dreams to Address Developmental Problems

*Riders on the storm,*
*Riders on the storm.*
*Into this house we're born.*
*Into this world we're thrown.*
*Like a dog without a bone,*
*An actor out on loan.*
*Riders on the storm.*

Jim Morrison, The Doors.

The dreams we have do not occur at random. Some dreams occur at important, even critical times in our lives. What follows are dreams that six people have had which reflect healing and supporting affects on their life's journey. I will use the dreams of people who have graciously shared their important life events and I shall explain the age-related life phase (Huber) and psychosocial task (Erikson) to illustrate the main challenge developmentally at that time of the dream. What I have discovered is that the developmental challenges put the dreams and AP aspects into a more succinct context for interpretation. I believe that consideration of the life context in which dreams occurred with the AP progressions and developmental challenges due to the age of the person enables more accurate interpretation of dreams to take place.

Please refer to Figure 10.1 on page 26 for identification of life phases and psychosocial tasks, giving the developmental contexts of Huber and Erikson outlined in this section with volunteer charts. Notice that there are twelve segments to the horoscope. Since it takes 6 years for the Age Point to go through each house, it is easy to determine by the age range in each house where the individual is and what developmental problems he/she has to address. For example, in house 5, the developmental phase of an individual of 25 will probably involve a love crisis and existential upsets, because this is the experience-testing phase of life. Using another example, a person of 68 will be dealing with issues of health and physical decline in the isolation and loneliness phase of life in house 12.

## Ann: Teen-Age Tragedy and Recovery.

*Age 16, 8 months– April 3, 1967.*

**Context:** Ann was driving and was in a car accident in which her girlfriend was killed. Subsequently, Ann suffered traumatic brain injury from the accident and it affected her mental processing and retention skills. Her high school senior year was academically challenging, because she had to teach herself how to learn her coursework with deficits from the accident. She had to relearn how to learn on her own, and she reported that her senior year was especially hard. It should be noted there were no neuropsychologists or crisis counselors in 1967, and Ann had to grieve the loss of her girlfriend on her own.

**The Dreams:** *'Realistic and detailed dreams. In my dreams, my girlfriend visits me to tell me she is OK and the accident wasn't my fault. Her visits were comforting. The dreams occurred in April every year after the accident. I don't know when the dream visits ended, mid-eighties maybe.'*

**Age Point Progression:** We will use three dates that Ann had this recurring visitation dream: April 1968; April 1969; April 1973. At the time of the accident Ann's progressed Moon Node Age Point was conjunct her natal Moon which was opposed to natal Uranus in the 10th house; this aspect is reflected by the initial shock to her body (head trauma) and the emotionally devastating impact of the loss of her friend (Figure 1.4).

**Developmentally:** Ann's age of 16 is consistent with Huber's life phase of Identity crisis which *'is focused upon difficulties in school and vocational development.'*[i] It is during Erickson's identity vs. role confusion psychosocial task which addresses the *'ego's ability to integrate previous identifications with the vicissitudes of the libido, with the aptitudes developed out of endowment and with the opportunities offered in social roles.'*[ii]

Ann would have had to find her ego identity through exploring and assimilating possible vocational roles via her education but the accident took a physical and emotional toll. These factors made the learning process more difficult. This time in her life was made doubly hard because her injury was consistent with a critical period of adolescent development. Subsequently, she had functionally recovered; later she became a teacher and an educational administrator.

**Aspects to Age Point:** Neptune, the Moon and Uranus are part of a linear connected aspect pattern in Ann's natal chart; these positions are aspected by her AP progressions and involved in a series of visitation dreams in the dates covered. It is revealing that Ann's unconscious

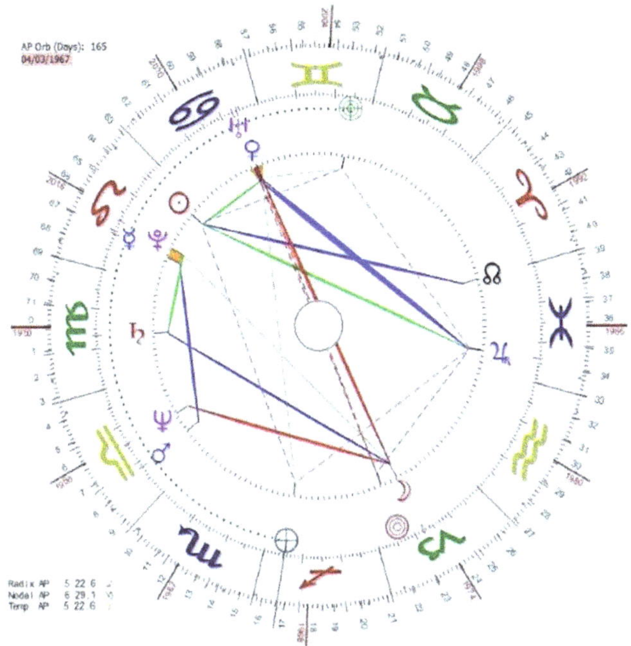


**Figure 1.4 Ann's radix chart showing AP at April 3, 1967**

*Cross hairs show position of radix AP in Sagittarius.*

motivation with this linear shaping of the planets involved the attainment of goals as a driving force.[iii]

In April 1968 during the first visitation dream, her progressed AP in Sagittarius was stressed before the 4th house; it was sextile natal Neptune in the 2nd house. During that dream her girlfriend visited her in a dream and told her she is okay, and the accident was not her fault. The AP was in a mutable sign in a mutable house, so it probably lessened Ann's guilt.

The dream in which the same message was conveyed to Ann by her girlfriend recurred in April 1969. At that time, progressed AP was in Sagittarius in the 4th house, was approaching conjunction to the moon node AP, and trine to natal Pluto conjunct Mercury in the 12th house. Ann probably had difficulty with conformity regarding family matters during this time, as her recovery was still in the foreground; she could not compromise with others (Sagittarius on cusp of 4th house).

In April 1973, her visitation dream reoccurred as Ann's progressed AP in Capricorn in the 4th house was conjunct her low point natal Moon in opposition to natal Uranus and Mercury in the 10th house.

Her feelings could be used constructively and directed into certain channels, as she continued to learn at school and recover (Capricorn is compatible with the water sign in the 4th house). Connections between the progressed AP and transcendental planets were evident in all the dates of her dreams. Her AP aspected her natal Pluto, which has *'to do with death and rebirth, with the transformation of one form of consciousness to another;'* with Neptune, which *'can provide the inner experiences we need to recognize the existence of something beyond the purely material…'* and with Uranus *'stimulating the desire to investigate what lies beyond our everyday world.'*[iv]

The visitation dreams comforted Ann, and their persistent frequency helped turn her grieving at the losses into resolved mourning, in which she was able ultimately to transcend the trauma and move on with her life.

## Rick: Birth of Self Confidence.

*Age 17 just before 18th birthday in 1966; and Age 19 in 1968*

**Context:**

**Dream 1.** Associations: *'I was back in my aunt's kindergarten class at age six, and colored the deer's antlers gold, and was laughed at by the kids.' I was in my senior year of high school and, having moved five times in my formative years, I was adjusting to returning to my home town. My cousin and I were friends and I was in a band and doing well academically. I had a girlfriend.'*

**Dream 2.** *'I was going to Penn State University and living with my parents. I had been in a band called the Young Lords and found my identity more as a musician writing and playing than as a student at that time. I had a girlfriend and we were going steady.'*

**Dream 1:** 1/1966. *'In the dream, I saw a stag with golden antlers soar across a lake. Then I saw a pachyderm soar across the same lake.'*

**Dream 2:** 2/1968. *'I was at a lake again. I walked into it not knowing what I might step on… rock, glass, and oozing mud. Weeds wafted around and touched my legs. I walked further into the lake, unafraid.'*

**Age Progression:**

**Dream 1.** The AP is on the cusp of the 4th house in Leo, in opposition to natal Sun in Aquarius in the 10th house. The AP and moon node AP are in opposition on the cusps of the 4th and 10th houses. The Sun is at the angle of two ambivalence triangles in Rick's natal chart, which predisposes him to look at life in black and white, in terms of either/or. Leo on the cusp of the 4th house shows that, at this time,

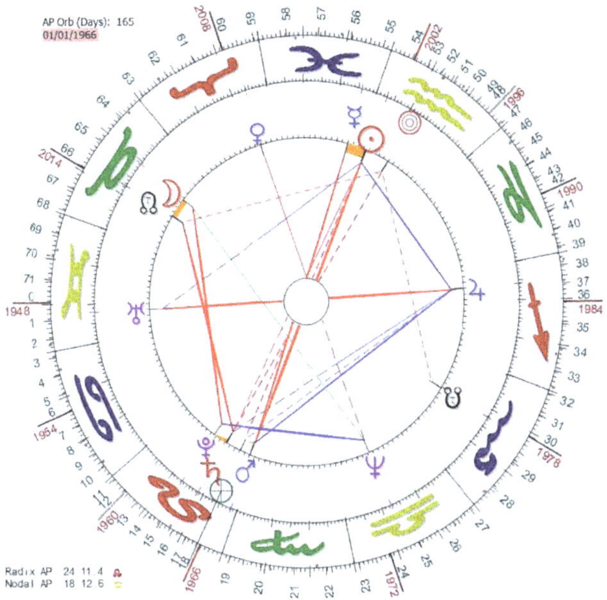


**Figure 2.4 Rick's radix chart showing AP just before age 18**

his goals conflict with the emotional claims of others, and the dream reflects this disconnect (Figure 2.4).

**Dream 2.** The AP transit is near the balance point in Virgo, in the 4th house, and trine to Rick's natal Moon in the mutable zone of the 11th house. The Moon is at the stimulating red/green angle of a large learning triangle whose retrograde direction might slow down the learning process. In this case, Rick's feelings are given an aim, and can be employed constructively (an earth sign in a water house). The peaceful trine from the AP adds substance to his over-stimulated natal Moon and could have helped with his confidence.

These dreams form a succession from Rick's perceiving of a stag with golden antlers soaring across a lake, along with an elephant doing the same to him being in the lake himself. Movement and energy are focused on individuality as opposed to Rick's collective family. He is challenged to think independently in a way that might lead to self-development but, in dream 1, he is an observer; he is ambivalent about moving forward. In dream 2, Rick at age 19 is preparing to leave home; he is spontaneous and feeling confident about his relationships with friends. He is getting good feedback from his environment: his grades at college are passable, his experience in the band, *Young Lords*, is good, and his relationship with his girlfriend is continuing. He is learning that his contacts with others give good feedback and feels optimistic. His independence is in harmony with his self-esteem and his need to be on his own.

**Developmentally:**
In dream 1, at age 17, Huber says that on the cusp of the 4th house, one's individuality comes to the foreground, and Rick has a vision of strong and independent movement (Stag and Elephant soaring over a lake). He is awakening to higher educational and intellectual interests, and self-realization on the individuality axis across houses 4 and 10.

In dream 2, at age 19, Rick is actually participating in the process of separating himself from his family (he now is in the lake) and supporting his independent lifestyle through the money he earns from the band.[v] His self-confidence is strengthened considerably, as he is not afraid of the unknown (symbolized by going through the lake, with the mud, weeds, rocks and grass wafting against his legs).

What appears as ambivalence in the first dream, with a glimpse of strength and independence, becomes clear involvement with reality in the second dream. Within two years, the AP stimulates the large learning triangle, involving the Moon and Pluto, which transforms his emotional confidence at a deep level as Rick expresses his artistic identity (Neptune in the 5th).

## Brittany: Liberation from a Haunting.

*Age 28 years and 6 months. Dream date 12/21/2016.*

**Context:** *'I just started back to work Monday the 19th after being off for maternity leave since August 12th 2016. Ryan (husband) and I fought a lot over the weekend prior to my starting back to work. Fought about his parents, Addison (new born daughter) being sick a lot, and Ryan's sleep/work schedule in his work with the railroad. I can't really connect how this dream is related to this other than the feeling of stress and myself trying to attempt to get Ryan's attention to subjects in our lives that are difficult.'*

**Dream:** *'12/21/2016. I fell asleep around 12:45 am. 1am, woke up with my heart pounding, trying to scream for Ryan, as I was also doing in the dream. Dreamt our friend Rich was seeing a girlfriend with children, and he had spirits attached to him who constantly messed with kids (girlfriend's). The kids wanted to be at their mom's house not Rich's, to be away from the dead people. I then saw the spirits they were talking about at Rich's in a separate room. Ryan was with me and he didn't see them. A dead woman in her twenties and her mother kept trying to touch me and grab me.'*

*Ryan and I had to walk from their house home. Rich's girlfriend and kids did too. We walked to our place which was far way. It was hot out but there was also ice on the roads and sidewalks, so we had to be careful. I was wearing a tank top, Capris and sneakers. When I would look to my right, I could see my reflection in windows and I could see my tank top change from a black and blue one to a whitish red tank top.*

*Rich's girlfriend's house ended up being two blocks down from where my mom's house is. They were going into the home. I yelled to the girlfriend who is an acquaintance of mine, who in real life doesn't know Rich at all. I said I could see who her kids saw—the ghosts. She said the kids never want to play in the yard at his house because of them, but they played in the yard here. She didn't seem fazed by it which made me feel like maybe she doesn't see what they do, but I now do.*

*It was Christmas time in my dream, when Ryan and I walked away from them. When they went inside I said I was sad those kids would have to spend their Christmas at his house, scared. Ryan agreed, and seemed to make me think he could see them too.*

*When Ryan and I got home (not our house, I didn't see the house we went into), I laid in bed and said to Ryan how I think these spirits are attached to Rich not the house. I turned my head to the side and saw the two women walking up the stairs and into my bedroom. There were three other adult people with them. They climbed onto my bed and kept touching me and laughing while I tried screaming for Ryan. He didn't see them or hear me. I forced myself awake. I was lying in real life how I was lying in bed in the dream. I could feel in my throat and mouth I was trying to yell in real life for Ryan as I was yelling in the dream.'*

**Age Point Progression and Aspects:** I will use December 21, 2016, when Brittany had this dream, as the reference point for AP progression. At this time, the AP transit is in Sagittarius, approaching conjunction to the stressed Uranus/Saturn conjunction before the 6th house cusp, in opposition to the natal Venus/Mercury conjunction stressed before the 12th house cusp (Figure 3.4). The AP in the 5th house *'represents peak efficiency and compromise with arranging her life, but can mean presumption and her trying to bring every one down to the same level.'* [vi] Her inner temperament finds confirmation in the outside world and does not need to adjust to it (Sagittarius in the 5th is fire sign in a fire house). This AP approaching conjunction with the Uranus/Saturn conjunction in opposition to Venus/Mercury, all of them stressed planets forming part of a linear connected shaping in her horoscope, reinforces her will to be directed toward the survival of her goals for her family. The AP's approach to conjunction with

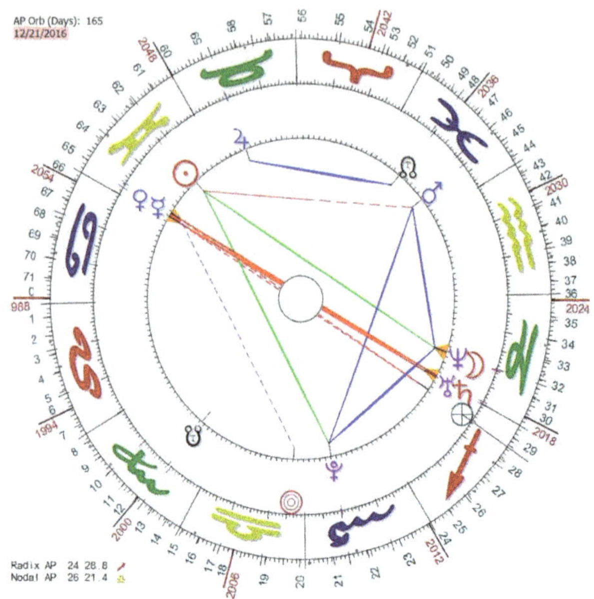


**Figure 3.4 Brittany's radix chart showing AP at age 28½**

the cusp on the Survival Axis (houses 6 and 12) makes the issues for Brittany more nerve-racking and shocking at this time.

**Developmentally:** The AP is in the phase (Huber) of maximum physical performance yet also approaching the 6th house of service. *"This is a time of highest power, speed and dexterity. Achievements are critically evaluated by others. All efforts are strategically planned to show how well life demands have been met. Here are the first results of individual striving in the professional and private sectors."*[vii]

Brittany will be judged by others by the way she opens up and uses her creative intelligence in the service of others. This is a tall order. Erikson's stage of *Intimacy vs. Isolation* emerges as the developmental struggle here when the AP is in the 5th house (Figure 1, page 3). *'Emerging from the search for identity, the young adult is eager and willing to fuse her identity with the identity of others resulting in intimacy… The counterpart of intimacy is the readiness to isolate when one has to differentiate between the familiar and the foreign thus destroying those forces and people whose essence seems dangerous to one's own, and whose territory seems to encroach on the extent of one's intimate relations.'*[viii]

The dream refers to intrusion by alien forces which threaten Brittany and her family's survival. The 'ghosts' in the dream may refer to her in-laws who have neither the competence to deal with her newborn, nor the same values as Brittany. She and her husband have arguments about her trying to keep his parents away from the baby until they learn how to care for Addison. Brittany is frustrated because Ryan's parents don't seem motivated to learn from her how to care for her daughter. And Ryan does not see her side of the situation but blames Brittany for shutting his parents out of the relationship with their granddaughter. But Brittany is holding her own and seems to be correct in doing so, since she is the main caretaker of her daughter and other family members may just have to adapt to her needs at this time.

### Judy: Assertive Re-orientation.

*Age 43 years and 11 months. Dream date July 3, 1992.*

**Context:** Judy's family had just moved to their new house the year before, in 1991. They had a new mortgage and had some financial problems. They had to reverse some commitments financially during this time and downsize. In July 1992, the family went to stay for a week at the Jersey seashore, staying with some friends in their house. Judy and her husband, John, were aware that their friends were wealthy in that they had a home at the shore and other resources. Their friends' husband had not had steady employment; he lived off his income from investments, worked for his family, and there was his wife's salary as a teacher. Judy's family also visited John's cousin that summer; he had just completed his Ph.D. and was successful in his new job as a school administrator. John was in a low status job on a hospital surgical floor as a social worker. Because of competition with John's male friends, who seemed successful, it bothered John (more than Judy) that they wanted to deal with material items in their house, like painting and upgrading the old house. They had to find the money to do it, and John's mother helped. His mother had expectations that they would be established in a nice home that was of upper middle class standard. Judy was much less concerned about the appearance of the house and status than John or his mother. All of the family's financial decisions about how to spend money were made jointly. But John was much more ambitious to improve their outward status than Judy was, probably due to his comparisons with friends, their financial problems, and his low status job. Sometimes Judy felt that John was making all the decisions and she was just going along with him.

**Dream 1:** *'I dreamed that John and I were visiting his nephew, and I was sitting outside in the porch. I heard John start discussing cars and how he was ready to buy a new one. I walked right into the kitchen where they were talking. I motioned for John to follow me. I was smiling and totally in control of myself. I screamed, when am I going to make a big money decision in this marriage? I said, 'I'm leaving. I may be home and I may not when you get home.'*

**Dream 2:** *'John took me up the street to show me a new house that he wanted to buy.'*

**Age Point Progression and Aspects:** Judy's AP transit was in Virgo applying to a conjunction of her natal Mercury conjunct Saturn in her 8th house (Figure 4.4). The AP transit is applying to a conjunction with Nodal AP transit, which was exact at 9 degrees Virgo on May 1993. This represents chiefly a desire for security, hanging onto our gains with resistance though inflexibility to new things and ability to communicate the need to trim one's sails.[ix]

At every new turn of events, this resistance concerns spending their joint resources and threatens Judy's sense of security. But, during this time her feelings are given space and can be employed constructively

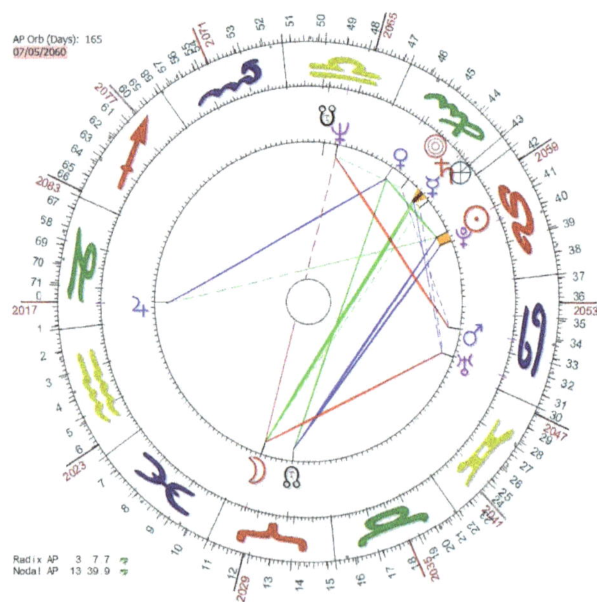


**Figure 4.4 Judy's radix chart showing AP at age 43 years 11 months**

(AP in earth sign on a water house). This transit of the AP conjunction with Saturn and Mercury also stimulates Judy's large learning triangle retrograde, which picks up her wanting to communicate her feeling values. She is stimulated by this transit to learn not to feel guilty and not to avoid conflict when she asserts her feeling values that her husband should not buy a new car.

**Developmentally:** The AP transit is on the cusp of the 8th house which Huber calls *'the new orientation in marriage, family and profession'*. This period often brings decisive changes in personal and professional sectors. As John and Judy's children become more independent, there is an awakening of intellectual and spiritual energies in Judy.

*'The serious problem of the meaning of life becomes important and manageable.'*[x] For Erikson, this period is marked by mid life crisis and *'the meeting of bodies and minds leading to a gradual expansion'* of (Judy's) ego-interests and investment in that which is being generated.[xi] The awakening of Judy's values and resistance to spending money that could cause financial stress seems to be the crux of this crisis time for her.

The dream of Judy's voicing opposition to a new car that John wants and taking a stand dramatizes Judy's egoic need for assertion of her values (in this case conservation of resources) to the point of separation from others if need be.

## Marilyn: Surgical Wounding and Promise of Healing.

*Age 52 years and 7months. Dream date October 18, 1999*

**Context:** On 11/02/1999, Marilyn was in hospital having an operation to sever the nerve to her right breast following a previous mastectomy and reconstruction (having used a muscle from her back to form the reconstruction), as it had been causing a problem. Afterwards, in the recovery room coming around from the anesthetic, she became aware that 'they,' the nursing staff, had wheeled in beside her another patient who had obviously also had an anesthetic (the energy pressure on the chest?). When Marilyn finally came around properly, back on the ward with a nurse attending her, she discovered to her horror that her right arm was paralyzed; only her hand would move. She told the nurse who looked very worried and said she would tell the surgeon. Marilyn was petrified that they had cut the wrong nerve.

The surgeon duly arrived and tried to reassure her, explaining that in order to find the right nerve to cut, they had touched the nerve to Marilyn's arm which must have bruised it. But, because her arm jerked when they touched it they knew it was the wrong nerve to cut. Remembering her dream, and realizing the connection, she took great comfort that, in this dream. Marilyn had been able to move her arm eventually. Happily that was true, but it took a scary three weeks for her to regain the use of that arm.

**Dream:** 10/18/1999. *'I had a dream that was so vivid that I really felt I was awake. I dreamt that I was lying in my bed and was feeling a great pressure of "energy" bearing down on my chest. Then "they," (there always seem to be nameless 'they' in dreams), wheeled into the room beside me a person lying on another bed. I somehow "knew" that this person also had the same uncomfortable sensation of pressure on her chest. Then I tried to move my right arm in order to get my arm out and over the duvet, but found I couldn't move it. All I could do was move my hand. Gradually I managed with just that hand to pull the duvet down until my arm was free of the covers. Then I discovered I could move my arm and woke up.'*

**Age Progression and Aspects:** The AP progression was in the 9th house in Leo conjunct the Nodal AP progression and opposed to the natal conjunction of Mercury and Mars in the 3rd house (Figure 5.4). The AP and Nodal AP progressions activated her Projection Figure, or Yod. Mercury conjunct Mars forms the meeting point of this Projection Figure and projects the qualities of Neptune (seeing other worlds) and Pluto (transformation and reconstruction) onto a 'screen' in her dream dramatizing the issue. As the AP and Nodal AP stimulated the apex of her Projection Figure and Marilyn was

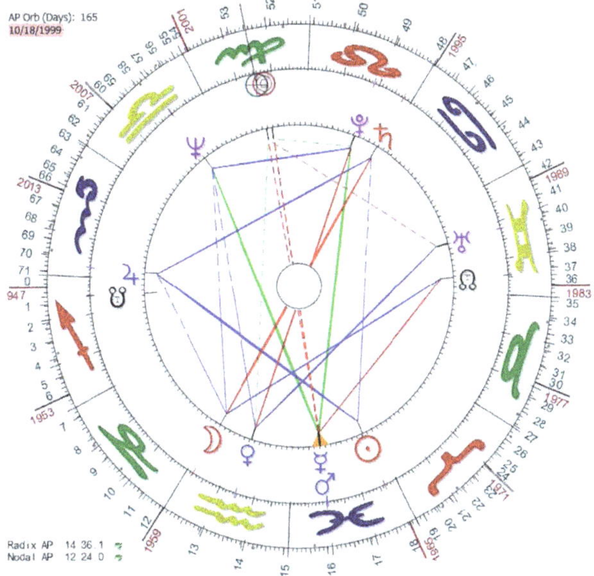


**Figure 5.4 Marilyn's radix chart showing AP at age 52 years 7 months**

conscious of her dream, she was able to foresee the future result of her operation, and that she would eventually get full movement of her arm. This dream gave her much comfort when she actually had to face the temporary paralysis of her arm.

**Developmentally:** The 9th house context concerns the meaning of life, "where from and where to." Huber indicates that the essential themes of the 9th house are self-determination and consciousness of our true destination. *'Those who can successfully reach this plateau of understanding will transcend their everyday problems.'*[xii] Marilyn's consciousness of this dream, recollected and remembered, was a great asset after the operation in coping with her temporary paralysis, because she had dreamed that this lack of functioning would not last. Her dream turned out to be true. Her faith must have grown because she could depend on her dreams to guide her through this crisis. This ability to work with dreams is part of her philosophy of life, is important, and can lead to a sense of controlling with her destiny. With these gifts to foresee the future through dreams, Marilyn would, as Erikson asserted, have developed integrity by tapping her unconscious with the result that she was able to transcend despair at a temporary loss of functioning.[xiii]

## John: Presage of a Passing.

*Age 51 years, 1 month, 2/9/2000*

**Context:** John's 92-year-old mother's health was failing. She lived with his sister, some 500 miles away from John's home. John spent two weeks with her, in August 2000, staying with his mother while his sister took a vacation from her care. John's mother continued to deteriorate in health and, in November 2000, she was admitted to a nursing home. She was there for 3 months, until she died of old age due to a descending aortic aneurysm of the heart, on February 13, 2001.

**Dream 1:** 2/9/2000. *'I heard a voice saying, "I will come like a thief in the night." Later the image of a general with a bald head and in full uniform appeared. He asked, "I heard there is a conflict down there." I said, "Yes." Associations: II Peter verse 10: "But the day will come as a thief in the night in which the heavens shall pass away with great noise and the elements shall melt with fervent heat; the earth also and the works also that are in it shall be burnt up."'*

**Dream 2:** 7/7/2000. *'A friend mentioned that we had a situation in which Jim's (our mutual friend) generous projects that he was doing for others paralleled Jacob's ladder. He pointed out that Jim was building a ladder to heaven and his life reflected that. And he also mentioned that "the fall of man" is reflected in Jim's life too.'*

**Dream 3:** 9/10/2000. *'I left a large group of people with this man. We walked across a meadow until we came to a river we had to cross. He pointed his finger and turned the water into ice (so we could cross). I was skeptical saying that I could not believe he could do this because downstream all the heat accumulated in the fire places would prevent it. But that was not the case.'*

**Age Point Progression and Aspects:** John's Nodal AP was progressing through Leo, and made a conjunction to natal Pluto stressed before the 9th house cusp, while the AP in intercepted Virgo was moving toward the low point of the 9th house. The progression of the AP forms the apex of an observant Eye figure with two transcendent planets, natal Neptune and natal Pluto making a sextile. At this time, John was moving confidently toward his goals in an unerring manner (earth sign AP in a fire house). Information from the Eye is received by John from Pluto on the unexpected death and rebirth, as well as from Neptune with connections with other worlds beyond the material plane.[xiv] This information is managed (in the context of triggering John's natal double ambivalence figure) by association

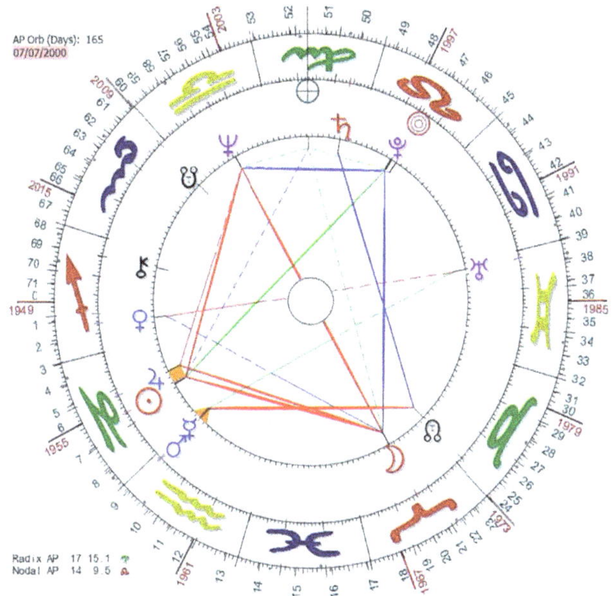


**Figure 6.4 John's radix chart showing AP at age 51 years 6 months**

with his mother's life through his religion-based dreams, being true to himself, and being loyal to her by going to see her unannounced one last time, two days before her death (see Figure 6.4).

**Developmentally:** Huber identified this time as the philosophical phase of life in which it is essential to find true values for one's existence. We often find interest in occult, magical, esoteric or spiritual disciplines as means for finding an understanding of life.[xv] Ego integrity vs. Despair is this task in which it is the ego's accrued assurance of its proclivity for order and meaning. This conveys an experience of some world order and spiritual sense beyond the selfish ego.[xvi]

On the other hand, despair expresses the feeling that time is short for an attempt to start a new life and we can mourn the fact that time is running out. But John's series of dreams convey that… (death) 'will come like a thief in the night'… there are right and wrong ways to get to heaven… and that one can develop spiritual values to transmute skepticism (symbolized by disbelief at the miracle of changing water to ice) into faith, helping us and others cross the great river Styx into the underworld.

The weekend before his mother's death, John got an intuition to get in the car and drive the 500 miles to visit his mother at the nursing facility. He left home alone and spent the weekend communing one last time with his mother. John came out of this experience facing his mother's death, on February 13, 2001, with stronger spiritual values, and faith that life continued after death. Although John's mother was not having a medical emergency the weekend before her death, John received the strong impression that he must visit her. He was grateful he listened to that 'still small voice within' and left to visit her. Her death was celebrated as a life fully lived, not grieved, because, at 94, her passing was natural and a higher world awaits.

# Chapter 5. Astrological Psychology Consultation

## Using Dreams and Developmental Contexts

*He's a real nowhere man*
*Sitting in his nowhere land*
*Making all his nowhere plans for nobody.*
*Doesn't have a point of view.*
*Knows not where he's going to*
*Isn't he a bit like you and me.*
*Nowhere man please listen*
*You don't know what you're missing.*
*Nowhere man. The world is at your command.*

Beatles, Lennon/McCartney

I have covered methods for dream recovery and hopefully spurred motivation for you to work hard with dreams because they can yield valuable discoveries on your life journey. I provide dream interpretation with Astrological Psychology's developmental phases as early in the life cycle as dream content can be recalled by my clients. Some of the dream discoveries can be life-changing to your view of what constitutes the real vs. the uncanny aspects of life.

There are four classes of dreams that are recorded by our volunteers in Chapter 4: visitation dreams, dreams revealing the unconscious presence of the shadow, dreams as compensation for a one-sided unconscious complex and precognitive dreams.

For Ann her dream, **Teenage Tragedy and Recovery**, is a Visitation Dream,[i] and is common in people who have had a traumatic experience. Dr. Alan Botkin documented Vietnam combat veterans who experienced visitations from deceased comrades who would reassure them that they were okay after being killed in war.[ii]

In Rick's dream of **Birth of Self Confidence** small boys are making fun of his drawing, and his subsequent hidden motive for wading into life's waters with the desire to dominate his fears of avoiding challenges is representative of his shadow side.[iii] Often the shadow side can give breadth to the personality, awakening potential that is missing in developing egos.

Brittany's **Liberation from a Haunting** confronts the dreamer with developmental challenges to rid herself of dependent people who prevent her from caring for her infant in a new mothering role and re-entering the work world after her pregnancy. This was also a shadow dream which prompted Brittany to be firm and dismiss those who stood in the way of her goals for herself and her infant daughter.

Judy's dream **Assertive Re-Orientation** was an awakening of a complex of Dominance/Submission deep in Judy's personal unconscious. She was one-sided in being too submissive to her husband but during a mid-life crisis, she was prompted by this dream to become more assertive and dominant in the relationship with her husband.[iv]

Marilyn's dream of having a precognitive dream where she saw a post surgical procedure paralyze her arm but become fully functional with time. This dream demonstrated a **Surgical Wounding and Promise of Healing** which enhanced her feeling of profound guidance and positive meaning in her values of her life.

John had received dreams that were precognitive of the passing of his mother which had implications for how death comes as a thief in the night and causes profound changes in survivors' world view. **Presage of Passing** dreams were representative of precognitive dreams.[v]

As a person develops an identity around 18 years of age, leaves home and engages in intimate relationships in the early twenties, dream interpretation can be invaluable, yielding its treasures to support ego growth and integration. Later in life, it is a useful tool on the job, with partnerships, during the mid-life crisis and while growing older, leading to retirement from active life. Ego integration (identification and support of ego planets) is so important to the successful completion of life tasks because of the need for a confident base for meeting one's needs of healthy self-esteem.

The model of sub-personalities is useful for helping to differentiate between *wants* and *needs*. Discernment of the differences between wants and needs is a necessary step in re-directing the desires and passions of the sub-personalities. Following the will of sub-personalities has more to do with wants than needs; giving in to the distractions you get from achieving the gratification of your needs. For ego integration to occur, you are advised to follow your needs rather than your wants. They are: needs for physiological states to be satisfied, needs for security and safety, needs for belonging, needs for self-esteem and, finally, needs for self-actualization. Although you should respect the desires of the sub-personalities, because they give breadth and depth to your personality, you are advised to put them in a secondary place because of their need for gratification.

I also want to help you to understand that the environment may block your ability to get adequate support from others (dynamic calculations). That situation may be one in which the environment does not recognize your talents through no fault of your own. When the environment does not support your temperament traits, you may feel like you are 'banging your head against a wall.' Reframing how to develop provides alternatives in adaptation to the environment is important to your adjustment to this life-long problem, if it effects you.

In addition, I want to provide support for those of you who have to deal with difficult initiation experiences through understanding the need for purification rituals. I also want to reframe what appear to be negative wounding experiences by seeing these challenges as rituals that have their benefits and actually can assist you to raise your consciousness; this is my purpose. But to do these interventions, it may be necessary to do a consultation for you.

It is not enough to provide an interpretation of the dream alone because one context is left out: where you are on the developmental cycle of growth throughout life. I have provided information on what the current daily real-life issues are that you face, and pointed out AP aspects to sensitive points in your horoscope that stimulate specific psychological drives and motivation at the time of the dream. Thus, these elements taken together—your dream, your daily life issues, your developmental challenges and opportunities, aspects of the AP to your sensitive ego planets, and aspect figures—are included in a complete dream consultation.

The number of life's challenges that happen may make you defensive when your ego attachments are threatened, and make you feel that you live in an insecure world. The helter-skelter of this era may not give you enough time to record inner dreams or interpret astrological psychology. This is an *Age of Anxiety* where there are rumors of terrorist attacks, wars and financial instability. You may be tempted to look outside yourself for safety and security. You may take refuge in the copious media outlets for distractions that pretend to transport you to a utopian world or, at worst, reinforce your cynicism about dystopia. Ultimately, however, each individual is responsible for finding meaning in her life and striving to live in the present moment.

Living in the 'eternal now,' as the existentialists recommend, is not for sissies. It takes courage to fulfill your need for self-realization and use your freedom to your full potential.[vi]

To transcend a healthy ego foundation and increase your awareness of different levels of consciousness is the goal of self-actualization. Few find their true, authentic selves in social institutions. But many do not find their true self by conforming to standards of creativity as prescribed by others. For it seems that once you are free of caring about what others want from you; when you live, create and strive for fulfilling your needs, then you can lose yourself in the present moment. You can become a true seeker and transcend the limits and distractions set upon you by age, education, or gender.

In life, fear of death scares people because of a threat of the death of the ego; and that is what makes spiritual development all the more important. What awaits you is an opportunity for a spiritual journey beyond ego attachments if you are mature and aware that independence exists. You can seize the opportunity to go beyond the routine world of security. Finding out what you are dreaming about and where you are on the life cycle of development helps you on this journey.

I hope I have given you a method through the application of astrological psychology principles and dream interpretation to find out how meaning can be a reality for you, the seeker. This book was so easily written because it was a joy to follow my bliss. This same process can lead the mystic in you on the road to individuation.[vii] In spite of outward distractions, going inside to discover a way to use dreams to guide you to greater self-actualization is a need that you may want to pursue.

## Consultation

I have an advanced diploma in the application of the theory of astrological psychology and do not deviate in my consultations from what the Astrological Psychological Association uses as guidelines for a consultation.[viii] I follow the presenting problem of my clients when they are asking for a consultation. I adhere to ethical guidelines of the National Association of Clinical Social Workers as a psychotherapist.[ix]

When I tell clients I do dream analysis, they may present their dreams and I use the forgoing method of analysis outlined in this book to provide self discovery to the challenges they present. Sometimes they do not want to work with dreams, so I will leave dream interpretation out but support ego integration, environmental/heredity dynamics, AP progressions and transits as they relate to why the client wishes to have an interpretation. I adhere to the principles of confidentiality, privacy and relative anonymity with my clients.[x]

Huber's AP progression emphasizes the phases of development and is much more specific than Erikson's *Eight Ages of Man*; Huber's model provides another context along with dream reporting and daily diaries to provide for rich dream interpretation. I believe this method of using dreams that I have presented is better than just using age point progression alone to address issues in clients' lives. Furthermore, in my view, this method of dream interpretation is accurate in identifying the guidance coming from the central core of the horoscope (which is the source of everything – Self and Divine entities). Although there are other ways of discerning divine guidance in addition to dreams, I have been only competent in dream guidance, so that has been the focus of my book.

My hope is that this book will attract seekers, psychologists, social workers, and astrologers who want to study the Huber method. This method of astrological psychology is superior to any method I have studied in my forty year career as an astrologer and psychotherapist. Furthermore, I hope I have scattered some seeds of enthusiasm for dreamwork because, in conjunction with Huber's method of age progression, it is a powerful tool. My clients tell me so and I believe them.

# Notes

## Notes to Introduction

i Huber, Bruno and Louise, *LifeClock, The Huber Method of Timing in the Horoscope*. Hopewell, Knutsford, England, 2006, p. 2.

ii Wikipedia, Developmental Psychology, Internet, 2016.

iii Erikson, Erik. *Childhood and Society*. W.W Norton and Company, New York, 1993, pp. 147-269.

iv Hopewell, Joyce, *Using Age Progression, Understanding Life's Journey*, HopeWell, Knutsford, England, 2013, p. 1.

v Ibid. p. 194.

vi Jung, Carl, *A Psychological Theory of Types*, Bollinger Series, Princeton, NJ, 1923, p. 706.

vii Ibid. p. 958.

viii Op. Cit. Huber *LifeClock*, p. 3.

ix Jacobi, Jolande, *The Psychology of C.G. Jung*, University Press, London,1973, pp. 106-107.

x Huber, Bruno and Louise. *LifeClock*, cover photo.

xi Huber, Bruno and Louse, *The Astrological Houses: A Psychological View of Man and His World*. Samuel Weiser, Inc. NY, 1998, p. 19.

xii Rogers, Kathy, "Timing in Your Life Journey: The Age Point in Huber Astrology", Astrological Association Conference, England. 2009.

xiii Huber, Bruno. *Astrological Psychosynthesis*. Hopewell, Knutsford, England, 1991, p. 129.

xiv Huber. *LifeClock*, Op. Cit. p. 55.

xv Ibid. p. 47.

xvi Hall, James *A. Jungian Dream Interpretation*. Inner City Books, Toronto, Canada, 1983, p. 28.

xvii Parfitt, Will. *Psychosynthesis and the Elements Beyond*, PS Avalon, Glastonbury, Somerset England, 2006, p. 216.

xviii Maslow, Abraham. *Religion, Values and Peak Experiences*, Penguin Books, NY, 1975, forward by E. Williams.

xix AA *Twelve Steps*, Step 1.

xx Maslow, Abraham, *A Theory of Human Motivation*, 2013. Watchmaker Publishing, Aberdeen and Washington, USA.

xxi Op. Cit. Parfitt, p. 129.

xxii Op. Cit. Parfitt, p. 114.

xxiii Op. Cit. Parfitt, pp. 117-118.

xxiv Ibid, p. 7, Psychosynthesis Egg Diagram.

## Notes to Chapter 1 Huber's Life Clock

i Lewis, Sue, *Astrological Psychology, Western Esotericism, and the Transpersonal*, Hopewell, Knutsford, England, 2015, p. 52.

ii Ibid.

iii Ibid.

iv Huber, *The Astrological Houses*, p. 19.

v Ibid. p. 21.

vi Ibid. p. 23.

vii Huber, *The Astrological Houses*, p. 60.

viii Huber, Bruno, Louise and Michael, *Aspect Pattern Astrology*, Hopewell, Knutsford, England, 2005, p. 104.

ix Huber, Bruno and Louise, *Life Clock*, Hopewell, Knutsford, England, 1986, p. 36.

x Author's italics. *The Field*, McTaggart, Lynn asserts that the universe is unified by an interactive field, based on apparent misunderstandings of physics.

xi Study Course in Diploma in Astrological Psychology, Module 1, Unit 3, Page 5. Chart Center.

xii Ibid.

xiii Op. cit. Huber, *Houses*, p. 24.

xiv Ibid. pp. 305-306.

xv Hopewell, Barry ed., *Astrological Psychology: The Huber Method*, Astrological Psychology Association, Hopewell Publishing, Knutsford, England, 2017, p. 227.

xvi Op. Cit. Rogers, "Timing in Your Life Journey".

xvii Op. Cit. Huber, *Life Clock*, p. 118.

xviii Huber, Bruno and Louise, *Transformation: Astrology and the Spiritual Path*, Hopewell, Knutsford. England, 2008, pp. 110-123.

xix Ibid. p. 67.

xx Op.Cit. Huber, *LifeClock*, pp. 204-205.

xxi Op. Cit. Rogers, "Timing in Your Life Journey."

xxii Ibid.

xxiii Erikson, Erik. *Childhood and Society* 1993 W. W, Norton, New York, New York.

xxiv Op. Cit. Huber, *Life Clock*, p. 44.

xxv Op. Cit. Erikson, pp. 247-258.

xxvi Op. Cit. Huber, *Life Clock*, pp. 49-50.

xxvii Op. Cit. Erikson, pp. 258-261.

xxviii Ibid. pp. 261-263.

xxix Ibid. p. 286.

xxx Op. Cit. Erikson, pp. 263- 266.

xxxi Op. Cit. Huber, *Life Clock* p. 55.

xxxii Ibid. p. 45.

xxxiii Op. Cit. Erikson, pp. 268-269.

xxxiv Op. Cit. Huber, *LifeClock*, p. 58.

xxxv Ibid. 47.

## Notes to Chapter 2 Life Tasks and going Beyond

i Assagioli, Roberto. *Transpersonal Development: the Dimension Beyond Psychosynthesis*. Smiling Wisdom; Inner Way Productions. Forres, Scotland. 2007. p. 16.

ii *Military Times*, August 19, 2015.

iii Geddes, John R; Miklowitz, D. J; *Lancet*. 2013 May 11. P. 381 (9878).

iv Op. Cit. Assagioli. *Transpersonal Development* .p. 7.

v Hillman, James. *Healing Fiction*. Spring Publications. Putnam, Conn. USA. 1994. pp. 54-55.

vi Op Cit. Parfitt, *Psychosynthesis,* p. 129.

vii Ibid.

viii Langs, Robert, MD, *Rating Your Psychotherapist*, Ballantine Books, NY, NY, 1989. p. 209.

ix Rogers, Carl. *Client Centered Therapy,* The Riverside Press, Cambridge, Mass. 1951.

x Gordon, Thomas, *Parent Effectiveness Training*, Three Rivers Press, NY, NY, 2000.

xi Huber, Bruno, *Astrological Psychosynthesis: Astrology as a Pathway to Growth*, Hopewell, Knutsford, England, 1996. p.70.

xii Ibid.

xiii Jung, Carl, *Psychological Types*, NY: Harcourt Brace; London: Keagan Paul, 1923.

xiv https://www.boundless.com/psychology/textbooks/boundless-psychology-textbook/biological-foundations-ofpsychology-3/genetics-and-behavior-31/the-influence-of-genes-on-behavior-137-12672/

xv Saudino, Kimberly Ph. D. “Behavioral Genetics and Child Temperament”. *Journal of Behavioral Pediatrics*.

xvi Huber, Louise, *Reflections and Meditations on the signs of the Zodiac*, 1984, American Federation of Astrologers, inc. Tempe, Arizona.p. 21.

xvii Hopewell, Joyce. *The Living Birth Chart*, HopeWell, Knutsford, England, 2008, p. 94.

xviii Op. Cit. Assagioli. *Transpersonal Development*. pp. 87, 88, 89, 93, 95.

xix Progoff, Ira Ph.D. *At a Journal Workshop*. Inward Beholding, Penguin Putnam, NY, NY. 1992. p. 60.

xx Pascal, Eugene. *Jung to Live By*. Warner books. NY, NY. 1972. p. 122.

xxi *DSM-IV*. American Psychiatric Association. Glossary of Defense Mechanisms and Coping Style, APA Washington, D. C. 2005, p. 757.

xxii Sadhu, Mouni, *Meditation*, Wilshire Book Company, Hollywood, California, 1978. P. 61.

xxiii Kornfield, Jack, *Mind Like Sky Meditation*. 2016. 28 minutes.

xxiv Grove, John. *Dreams and Astrological Psychology*. Hopewell Publishing. Knutsford, England. 2014.

xxv Montagu, Ashy. *Man's Most Dangerous Myth*, Harper, NY, NY. 1942.

xxvi Op Cit. Grove, *Dreams*, p. 49.

xxvii Op.Cit . Assagioli, p. 94.

xxviii Huber, Bruno and Louise. *The Planets and their Psychological Meaning*, Hopewell, Knutsford, England, 2006, pp. 106-108.

xxix Ibid. pp. 111-112.

xxx Ibid. pp. 115-117.

## Notes to Chapter 3 Capturing Dreaming Events

i Ullman, Montague, "Guidelines for Teaching Dreamwork' p. 123 in *Dreamtime and Dreamwork* . Ed. Krippner, Stanley. Jeremy P. Tarcher, Inc. Los Angeles, California, 1990.

ii Ibid. p. 124.

iii Jung, C. G. *Dreams*, Bollingen Series, Princeton, NJ, 1974. p 98.

iv Van de Castle, Robert L., *Our Dreaming Mind*, Ballentine Books, NYC, NY.1994 p. 232.

v Ibid. p. 264.

vi Ibid. p. 233.

vii R. Weisz and D. Foulkes, "Home and Laboratory Dreams Collected Under Uniform Laboratory Sampling Conditions," *Psychophysiology* 6 (1970), pp.558-96.

viii Bose, V. S. C. *"Dream Content Transformations: An Empirical Study of Freud's Secondary Revision Hypothesis,"* Doctoral Dissertation, Andra University, Waltair India, 1982.

ix Globus, G. *Dream Life, Wake Life* , Albany NY: State University of New York Press, 1987, p. 21.

x Bohm, D. *Wholeness and the Implicate Order*, Routledge, London, 1980.

xi Op Cit. Globus, p.178.

xii Op Cit. Van de Castle, pp. 241-250.

xiii Ibid. p. 253.

xiv Carney, Coleen and Manber, Rachel. *Goodnight Mind*, New Harbinger Publications, Oakland, California, 2013, pp. 73-87.

xv Parfitt, Will, *Psychosynthesis: The Elements and Beyond*, PS Avalon, Glastonbury, England, 2006. p. 224.

xvi Ibid. p. 48.

xvii Ibid.

xviii Op Cit. Progoff.

xix Veterans Affairs Center for Stress Recovery. www.ptsd.va.gov. *Traumatic Nightmares and PTSD Treatment Through Imagery Rehearsal Therapy* (IRT).

xx Op Cit. Grove, *Dreams*, p. 52.

xxi Op. Cit. Ullman, Montague, in Krippner, Stanley ed. pp. 122-123.

xxii Op Cit. Hall, p. 120.

xxiii Ibid. p. 52.

xxiv Ibid. pp 32-33.

xxv Op Cit, Hopewell, Barry, *Astrological Psychology*, p. 38.

xxvi Op Cit. Huber, *LifeClock*, p. 46.

xxvii Ibid. p. 59.

xxviii Ibid.

xxix Bogzaran, Fariba, "Painting Dream Images" in *Dreamtime and Dreamwork* ed. Krippner, Stanley, Jeremy P. Tarcher, Inc. Los Angles, California, 1990, p. 117.

xxx Schulman, Martin, *Karmic Astrology: the Moons Nodes and Reincarnation*, Samuel Wiser, Inc. NY, NY, 1975. pp. 22-24.

xxxi Op. Cit. Ullman,Montague, in *Dreamtime and Dreamwork*, pp. 127-128.

xxxii Wilheim/Baynes, *The I Ching, Book of Changes*, Bollengen Foundation, NY, 1950, pp. 225-225. The Image, Joyous Hexagram #58.

## Notes to Chapter 4 Using Dreams

i Op Cit. Huber, *LifeClock*, p. 51.

ii Op Cit. Erikson, p. 161.

iii Op. Cit. Huber, *LifeClock*, p. 104.

iv Ibid. pp. 189-190.

v Ibid .p. 52.

vi Ibid. pp. 185-186.

vii Ibid. p. 53.

viii Op Cit. Erikson, pp. 263-264.

ix Op. Cit. Huber, *LifeClock*, pp. 182, 186.

x Ibid. p. 56.

xi Op. Cit. Erickson. p. 267.

xii Op. Cit. Huber, *LifeClock,* p. 57.

xiii Op. Cit. Erikson, p. 268.

xiv Op. Cit. Huber, *LifeClock,* pp. 189-190.

xv Ibid. p. 57.

xvi Op. Cit. Erikson. p. 268.

## Notes to Chapter 5 Astrological Psychology Consultation

i Grove, John. *Dreams and Astrological Psychology*, Hopewell Publishing, Knutsford, UK, 2014. p. 82.

ii Botkin Alan. *Induced After Death Communication.* Hampton Road Publishing. Charlottesville, VA, 2005.

iii Op. Cit. Grove, *Dreams*, p. 61.

iv Ibid, p. 85.

v Ibid, p. 55.

vi May, Rollo. *Man's Search for Himself,* W.W. Norton, London, 195, p. 169.

vii Campbell, Joseph, *Myths To Live By*, Bantam books, NY, NY, 1988, p. 221.

viii Hopewell, Barry, *Astrological Psychology*, p. 249.

ix National Association of Social Workers, USA, *NASW Code of Ethics.* 1996.

x Op.Cit. Hopewell, pp. 250-251.

# Selected Publications

### *Astrological Psychology, Western Esotericism and the Transpersonal*

by Sue Lewis (2015)

*HopeWell Publishing, Knutsford, UK*

Sue Lewis's scholarly account of Huber Astrological Psychology which has its roots in Western Esotericism and Transpersonal Psychology identifies the foundation principles on which the Swiss Pioneers Bruno and Louise Huber taught in their Astrological Psychology Institute. She has brought to us in this 200-page paperback, the history and development of the Huber School of Switzerland and linked it with the tradition of Western esoteric thought as applied to Astrological Psychology. Included is a description of our legacy of philosophical concepts on which these practices are based.

Sue has a long and devoted study, practice and teaching of Astrology since 1980 and earned many distinguished credentials in Transpersonal Psychology. She was awarded a Diploma in Astrological Psychology Institute (now the Astrological Psychology Association) in 2003. She graduated with an MA with Merit in Western Esotericism in 2012 from University of Exeter Centre for the Study of Esotericism. This book represents Sue's scholarly and seeker identities in full display and is essential reading for any serious student of Astrological Psychology.

## *Using Age Progression: Understanding Life's Journey*

by Joyce Hopewell, Principal Emeritus
of the Astrological Psychology Association (2013)

*HopeWell Publishing, Knutsford, UK*

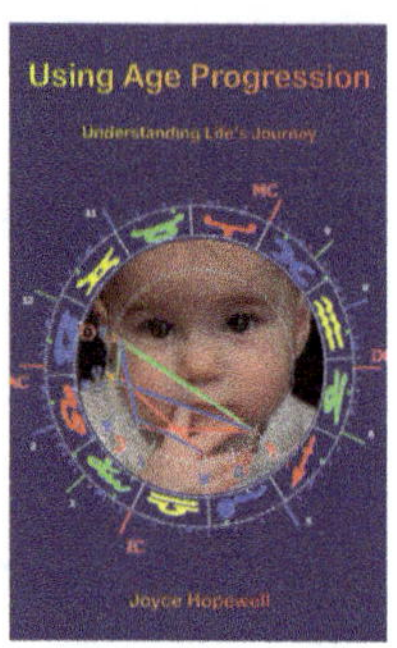


Joyce Hopewell's 4th publication on Astrological Psychology, *Using Age Progression* provides in paperback form with beautiful graphics an application of timing of psychological phases of development throughout the life cycle. It is essential reading for the newcomer to Astrological Psychology and the advanced practitioner.

*Using Age Progression* is beyond a doubt the most sophisticated method today using astrology and psychology to understand significant life experiences that are reflected in the birth chart based on exact time and place of birth.

As Joyce explains, Age Progression reflects in numerous examples, more the inner experience for the clients who use it rather than making predictions of coming events. She is a harbinger of a theoretical and scientific understanding and application of Astrological Psychology more so than traditional predictive astrology.

Joyce presents practical examples from real people explaining the meaning of aspects of the Age Point to sensitive areas of the horoscope at differing times in their lives as she highlights developmental challenges and opportunities. *Using Age Progression* is both technically adept and wonderfully descriptive of the process of psychological growth.

Joyce's other publications include, *The Cosmic Egg Timer* (2004); *The Living Birth Chart* (2008); and *Aspect Patterns in Colour* (2012).

www.ingramcontent.com/pod-product-compliance
Ingram Content Group UK Ltd.
Pitfield, Milton Keynes, MK11 3LW, UK
UKHW021827270726
14058UKWH00001B/29

9 780995 673618